MEATPACKERS

*An Oral History of Black Packinghouse Workers
and Their Struggle for Racial and Economic Equality*

Twayne's
ORAL HISTORY SERIES
Donald A. Ritchie, Series Editor

PREVIOUSLY PUBLISHED

*Between Management and Labor:
Oral Histories of Arbitration*
Clara H. Friedman

*Building Hoover Dam: An Oral
History of the Great Depression*
Andrew J. Dunar
and Dennis McBride

*Children of Los Alamos:
An Oral History of the Town
Where the Atomic Age Began*
Katrina R. Mason

*Crossing Over: An Oral History
of Refugees from Hitler's Reich*
Ruth E. Wolman

Doing Oral History
Donald A. Ritchie

*From the Old Country:
An Oral History
of European Migration to America*
Bruce M. Stave and John F.
Sutherland with Aldo Salerno

*Grandmothers, Mothers,
and Daughters: Oral Histories
of Three Generations
of Ethnic American Women*
Corinne Azen Krause

*Head of the Class: An Oral History
of African-American Achievement
in Higher Education and Beyond*
Gabrielle Morris

*Her Excellency: An Oral History
of American Women Ambassadors*
Ann Miller Morin

*Hill Country Teacher:
Oral Histories from the
One-Room School and Beyond*
Diane Manning

*The Hispanic-American Entrepreneur:
An Oral History
of the American Dream*
Beatrice Rodriguez Owsley

*Homesteading Women:
An Oral History of Colorado,
1890–1950*
Julie Jones-Eddy

*Infantry: An Oral History
of a World War II
American Infantry Battalion*
Richard M. Stannard

*Married to the Foreign Service:
An Oral History of the
American Diplomatic Spouse*
Jewell Fenzi with Carl L. Nelson

*Peacework: Oral Histories
of Women Peace Activists*
Judith Porter Adams

*Rosie the Riveter Revisited:
Women, the War, and Social Change*
Sherna Berger Gluck

*A Stranger's Supper:
An Oral History of Centenarian
Women from Montenegro*
Zorka Milich

*The Unknown Internment:
An Oral History of the Relocation
of Italian Americans
during World War II*
Stephen Fox

*Witnesses to the Holocaust:
An Oral History*
Rhoda Lewin

*Women in the Mines:
Stories of Life and Work*
Marat Moore

RICK HALPERN
ROGER HOROWITZ

MEATPACKERS

*An Oral History
of Black Packinghouse Workers
and Their Struggle
for Racial and Economic Equality*

TWAYNE PUBLISHERS
An Imprint of Simon & Schuster Macmillan
New York

PRENTICE HALL INTERNATIONAL
London   Mexico City   New Delhi   Singapore   Sydney   Toronto

Twayne's Oral History Series No. 25

Meatpackers
Rick Halpern and Roger Horowitz
Copyright © 1996 by Twayne Publishers

Twayne Publishers
An Imprint of Simon & Schuster Macmillan
1633 Broadway
New York, NY 10019-6785

Library of Congress Cataloging-in-Publication Data

Halpern, Rick.
    Meatpackers: an oral history of Black packinghouse workers and
their struggle for racial and economic equality / Rick Halpern,
Roger Horowitz.
        p.   cm. — (Twayne's oral history series)
    Includes bibliographical references and index.
    ISBN 0-8057-9120-5 (cloth)
    1. Afro-American packing-house workers—Interviews.   2. Afro
American packing-house worker—History—Sources.   3. Packing
houses—United States—History—Sources.   I. Horowitz, Roger.
II. Title.   III. Series.
HD8039.P152U54   1996
331.6'396073—dc20
                                                            96-25096
                                                            CIP

10   9   8   7   6   5   4   3   2   1

Printed in the United States of America

To the memory of Ralph Helstein,
UPWA President 1946–68,
who made this all possible

Preamble, United Packinghouse Workers of America Constitution

We recognize that our industry is composed of workers of all nationalities, of many races, of different creeds and political opinions. In the past these differences have been used to divide us and one group has been set against another by those who would prevent our unifying. We have organized by overcoming these divisive influences and by recognizing that our movement must be big enough to encompass all these groups and all opinions. We must always be alert and ready to strike down any attempt to divide us. We must destroy the possibility of disunity through the education of our membership in the spirit of solidarity with a view to eliminating all prejudices.

From *Proceedings, First Constitutional Convention of the United Packinghouse Workers of America, 1943,* 53.

Contents

Foreword

Before the Civil Rights Movement of the 1950s and 1960s, labor unions promoted social change, racial equality, and tolerance. They also offered minorities a chance to advance economically. For thousands of African Americans who left the Deep South in the early decades of the twentieth century, the meatpacking houses of the Midwest provided employment opportunities when other doors remained closed. Work in the packinghouses threw black laborers into contact with many white workers, particularly immigrant laborers, and introduced them to labor unions. Inadvertently, managerial policy in the packinghouses gave power and job mobility to African Americans by assigning them to work on the critical but less desirable "killing floors." Despite difficult working conditions on the floor, an internal line of promotion led to better pay and more secure employment for black men (since black women were excluded from the killing floors, they held poorer paying, less secure jobs). Conditions in the packinghouses fostered an unusual degree of interracial unionism and helped black workers advance from strikebreakers to strike-makers. The meatpackers' oral histories record the importance of their experience for African Americans in the Midwest and provide a remarkable model of the power of interracial cooperation in labor organizing and the larger society. Their voices are strong and their message is clear: in union there is strength.

Oral history may well be the twentieth century's substitute for the written memoir. In exchange for the immediacy of diaries or correspondence, the retrospective interview offers a dialogue between the participant and the informed interviewer. Having prepared sufficient preliminary research, interviewers can direct the discussion into areas long since "forgotten," or no longer considered of consequence. "I haven't thought about that in years" is a common response, uttered just before an interviewee commences with a surprisingly detailed description of some past incident. The quality of the interview, its candidness and depth, generally will depend as much on the interviewer as the interviewee, and the confidence and rapport between the two adds a special dimension to the spoken memoir.

Interviewers represent a variety of disciplines and work either as part of a collective effort or individually. Regardless of their different interests or the variety of their subjects, all interviewers share a common imperative: to collect memories while they are still available. Most oral historians feel an additional responsibility to make their interviews accessible for use beyond their own research needs. Still, important collections of vital, vibrant interviews lie scattered in archives throughout every state, undiscovered or simply not used.

Twayne's Oral History Series seeks to identify those resources and to publish selections of the best materials. The series lets people speak for themselves, from their own unique perspectives on people, places, and events. But to be more than a babble of voices, each volume organizes its interviews around particular essays that place individuals into the larger historical context. The styles and format of individual volumes vary with the material from which they are drawn, demonstrating again the diversity of oral history and its methodology.

Whenever oral historians gather in conference, they enjoy retelling experiences about inspiring individuals they met, unexpected information they elicited, and unforgettable reminiscences that would otherwise have never been recorded. The result invariably reminds listeners of others who deserve to be interviewed, provides them with models of interviewing techniques, and inspires them to make their own contribution to the field. I trust that the oral historians in this series, as interviewers, editors, and interpreters, will have a similar effect on their readers.

DONALD A. RITCHIE
Series Editor, Senate Historical Office

Preface

The United Packinghouse Workers of America Oral History Project

The narratives in this collection are the result of a massive oral history project conducted in the mid-1980s. Sponsored by the State Historical Society of Wisconsin (SHSW) and funded by a grant from the National Endowment for the Humanities, the United Packinghouse Workers of America Oral History Project aimed to supplement the written sources on work and unionism in the American meatpacking industry. The authors of this volume wrote the grant proposal and served as the project's paid staff and principal interviewers.

The interviewers were able to draw upon unusually extensive documentation on unionism in the meatpacking industry. The records of the United Packinghouse Workers of America (UPWA), the principal meatpacking union, are deposited at the SHSW and take up more than six hundred linear feet of space. However, the records focus on the institutional history of the international union and reveal relatively little about the lives of workers and their activities in local areas. Research in local newspapers and the records of the Congress of Industrial Organizations (CIO), the National Association for the Advancement of Colored People (NAACP), and the National Urban

League supplemented knowledge gleaned from the UPWA records, especially in respect to the many connections between the union and the civil rights movement. The interviews were designed to provide an alternative perspective by drawing upon the points of view of the workers themselves, and uncovering information and opinions unavailable in written sources. They also provided a means of assessing the union's claim to serve as a force for progressive social change in the workplace and in the community.

Potential interviewees were identified in two stages. First, key members of the union at the local level emerged as a result of research in archival sources. This investigation established a list of priority interviews. Second, project staff attempted to locate prioritized individuals through telephone books and local contacts. Of particular assistance were former UPWA members, many still active in retiree organizations, and officials of United Food and Commercial Workers (UFCW) local unions, the successor organization to the UPWA in the meatpacking industry. Often this second stage resulted in the identification of additional potential respondents who were important in their local unions and known among their peers as active, observant, and approachable individuals.

Most interviews were conducted jointly by Halpern and Horowitz in a union office, a private home, or a hotel room. Loosely structured interview agendas were based on preliminary phone interviews and research in written sources. Although particular questions varied, there were certain topics covered in all interviews, including information about packinghouse workers' communities, work and union activities, race relations, and the experiences of women and minority groups. Among the richest areas explored in these interviews were those pertaining to race relations in general, and the civil rights activities of the UPWA in particular.

In the course of the two-year project, 117 former UPWA members and 11 other individuals who had close contact with the union were interviewed. Of these interviewees, 85 were white, 42 were black, and 1 was a Mexican-American woman. There were 67 men and 18 women among the whites, 28 men and 14 women among the blacks. Tapes and detailed abstracts of all the interviews are deposited at the State Historical Society of Wisconsin, as are a number of interview transcripts. A complete guide to these interviews is included in the appendix.

Most of the interviewees were active in local unions and spent their working careers in a packinghouse. In addition, great effort was devoted to locating and interviewing spokespersons for different points of view within the UPWA. This book draws primarily from the interviews with black workers.[1]

The large number of oral history interviews in the UPWA collection made it necessary for the authors to choose only a portion for inclusion in this volume. Geography and interview quality were the most important criteria. Chicago and Kansas City represent important centers of the national meatpacking industry as well as large and dynamic black communities. Fort Worth introduces an important southern contrast. And Waterloo, Iowa, brings in the experiences of blacks in a small and predominantly white Midwestern town. The interview with Rowena Moore, the only one from Omaha included in the book, expresses a critical perspective on the UPWA's commitment to black rights and contains an extraordinary story.

Because of their length, we found it necessary to significantly edit these interviews. For example, the original Philip Weightman interview is over nine hours long, and the complete transcript runs to more than fifty thousand words. In the editing process we endeavored to keep the words, phrases, and texture of the interviews intact while trying to improve narrative flow and clarify meaning. The grammar, terminology, and sentence structure of the interviews have been retained so long as the passage was understandable. When widely separated parts of an interview touched on similar or related topics, we have brought those segments together. In the stories of Virginia Houston and William Raspberry, two interviews with each individual have been combined into a single narrative.

Acknowledgments

Oral history is an interpersonal experience whose product, the interview, is the result of the formal recorded dialogue between interviewer(s) and inter-viewee(s) and the conviviality established through informal conversations that never appear on the tape. Because oral interviews reflect the relationship between interviewers and interviewees, we want to specify the sociological and cultural differences between ourselves and the packinghouse workers who voices can be heard in this book. Two relatively youthful and educated white males from professional families, we interviewed working-class black men and women who were over 65 and generally had, at most, a high school degree.

Of course, in these dialogues, we made it clear that we were the students and they were the teachers. For the interviews to occur at all, these black men and women had to consent to meet with us and to trust us sufficiently to con-vey their views and experiences. It was their willingness to do so and to use the interviews to bridge the cultural differences between us that made this book possible. Our most important debt is to the workers who consented to be interviewed and whose narratives appear in this volume.

We also want to thank the former UPWA members who used their author-ity among other packinghouse workers to help arrange interviews. Les Orear, in his capacity as a former UPWA leader and president of the Illinois Labor History Society, opened many doors that without his intervention would have remained closed. In Chicago, Todd Tate not only shared his experiences in the Armour plant but also served as an intermediary for other interviews, along with two other former UPWA members, Eunetta Pierce and Richard Saunders. Frank Wallace played a similar role in Fort Worth, as did Lucille Bremer and Viola Jones in Waterloo and Max Graham in Omaha. Svend Godfredson, himself an important union founder from Austin, Minnesota, placed us in contact with Philip Weightman and persuaded him to meet with us. Terry Stevens arranged the wonderful interview with her father, Charles Pearson.

Longtime UPWA president Ralph Helstein (now deceased) and his wife, Rachel, deserve our thanks as well. As two nervous first-year graduate students at the University of Wisconsin, we were welcomed with open arms by the Helsteins when we approached Ralph for an interview in 1983. His encouragement stimulated us to prepare the successful grant proposal for the UPWA Oral History Project. After Ralph's death, Rachel remained an important supporter and booster of our work and arranged the interview with then Congressman Charles Hayes over a sumptuous dinner.

Since the oral history project had the support of the United Food and Commercial Workers (UFCW), local UFCW officials also were a great help. Ellen Newton in the UFCW's national office provided supportive and timely assistance, as did Rogers Farmer in Chicago and Paulia Weaver in Fort Worth.

Financial support for the interviews and their transcription was essential as well. A grant from the National Endowment for the Humanities allowed the State Historical Society of Wisconsin to sponsor the two-year UPWA Oral History Project. Additional interviews conducted by Roger Horowitz were aided by funding from the University of Wisconsin Graduate School and a Beveridge grant from the American Historical Association. A generous award from the Graduate School of Arts and Sciences at the University of Pennsylvania enabled Rick Halpern to return to Chicago for another intensive round of interviews. Funding to transcribe the interviews and to pay for other costs associated with the book were received from the Illinois Labor History Society, the Isobel Thornley Bequest of the University of London, and the British Academy. Susan Hutton, Rachel Aucott, Heather Latham, and Charmaine Harbort worked diligently to transcribe the often difficult interview tapes.

We also want to thank the sponsor of the oral history project, the State Historical Society of Wisconsin (SHSW), and its staff. State Archivist Gerald Ham lent his support to the project at its very early stages. His successor, Peter Gottlieb, arranged for the SHSW to grant permission for Twayne Publishers to publish the edited interviews. Archivist James V. Cavanaugh played a major role securing NEH funding through his critical reading of successive drafts of the grant proposal. Jim served as project director until departing to become president of the South Central Federation of Labor, AFL-CIO; we benefitted enormously from his considerable expertise as an oral historian. Archivist Donna Sereda skillfully edited the interview abstracts and prepared a detailed index. We also were fortunate that fellow graduate student Nancy MacLean was able to work on the project, conducting background research that helped prepare us for field interviews.

Several faculty members at the University of Wisconsin also played an important role in the oral history project. J. Rogers Hollingsworth merits special thanks for encouraging us to be ambitious and to apply for NEH funding. Herbert Hill, a participant in some of the events described in this book, served as project advisor. We benefited from his firsthand knowledge of the labor and civil rights movements and from his relentless, yet always constructive criticism of our work and ideas.

Finally, we would like to acknowledge that this book is the result of an unusual collaborative relationship that has spilled over fifteen years and two continents and has drawn into its vortex parents, spouses, and children. We have lived in the same place for a total of only three years, as Rick Halpern departed from Madison after receiving his master's degree and then returned for fourteen months during the UPWA Oral History Project. Once he obtained employment in London, the greater expanse of the Atlantic Ocean separated us. Nonetheless, the intense experience of jointly conducting research in archival collections and departing on weeklong expeditions to conduct oral interviews forged a lasting intellectual comraderie that continues to defy distance.

Maintaining our collaboration, though, has required the support of our families. Roger's mother, Louise Horowitz, drew on her experience as a professor of philosophy to provide critical advice for the initial drafts of the oral history grant proposal. At times, our parents were pressed into service to fill more mundane tasks as couriers or mail drops. Our spouses, Beth Landau and Marie Laberge, interrupted their own lives to facilitate the few short, intense visits we could afford. Along with our parents, they also provided important intellectual critiques of our work at key points in its development. And our children, who remained blissfully ignorant of why their daddies were so busy, reminded us always why the workers we interviewed had struggled so hard to form organizations that could produce a better future for us all.

Rick Halpern, University College London
London, England

Roger Horowitz, Hagley Museum and Library
Newark, Delaware

I

"THE STRENGTH OF THE BLACK COMMUNITY"
African American Workers, Unionism, and the Meatpacking Industry

The strength of the black community was in men working in steel mills and packinghouses, steady jobs. They were the real role models. There were a few doctors and lawyers. They were helpful, of course. But what really made the neighborhood stable was the fact that the men were working all the time.

—Reverend C. T. Vivian, 1992[1]

During the Great Migration of the 1910s, it was often the hope of securing gainful employment in meatpacking that fired the dreams and imagination of southern blacks seeking to escape the limits imposed by rural poverty, sharecropping, and Jim Crow segregation. One migrant from Mississippi later recalled, "The packinghouses in Chicago for awhile seemed to be everything. You could not rest in your bed at night for Chicago." The names of packinghouse firms such as Swift and Armour were familiar to southern migrants, because these and other large packers sold their products in branch houses and butcher shops throughout the South. As they considered following friends and relatives north, letters sent back from places like Chicago encouraged them to look for work in meatpacking. "I am doing well," one woman wrote to friends in Alabama. "I work in Swifts packing Co. in the sausage department. . . . Tell your husband work is plentiful here."[2]

By the 1920s, the wages earned by African Americans in meatpacking provided a foundation for many Midwestern black communities. Black packinghouse workers, despite the onerous conditions under which they labored, were respected and valued members of their community. In a labor market that severely restricted black opportunity, packinghouse jobs were among the best available for black men and women. Their wages underwrote vital community structures, including businesses, churches, fraternal orders, and cultural institutions. The black experience in meatpacking is central to understanding the growth, development, and vitality of black urban life in twentieth-century America.[3]

Packinghouse employment also placed blacks in an unusual interracial environment. In the plants, they joined recent East European immigrants, older Irish, Scandinavian, and German stock, along with native-born Protestant workers. The resulting mixture of racial and ethnic groups at work contrasted sharply with the rigid practice of racial segregation in housing, employment, and access to services enforced by Jim Crow legislation in the South and powerful informal customs in the North. Indeed, in many urban areas the packinghouse was the largest interracial institution, one of the few places where blacks and whites interacted on a daily basis.

The integrated character of the packinghouse workforce made it impossible for unions and union advocates to avoid the issue of race. Tensions marked the initial encounter between black packinghouse workers and labor organizations. African Americans who had experienced the racially discriminatory policies of unions affiliated with the American Federation of Labor (AFL) eschewed labor organizations in the early twentieth century. The small minority of black workers who joined unions in Chicago and other industrial centers during World War I faced taunts such as "You are nothing but a lot of white folks' niggers" from their own race. The exclusionary policies of the AFL, and the anti-union sentiment this engendered among blacks, made African Americans a ready strikebreaking force for the packing companies, further inflaming racial enmity. "The white butchers hated the Negroes because they figured they would scab on them when trouble came," recalled black packinghouse worker Elmer Thomas.[4]

It was not until the 1930s that an organizing drive under the aegis of the Congress of Industrial Organizations (CIO) was able to persuade blacks that unionism could serve the interests of all workers, not just whites. Far from being reluctant converts, blacks were often the driving force in the formative unions and were able to use these labor organizations to ameliorate racial prejudice. "I'll always believe they done the greatest thing in the world getting everybody who works in the yards together, and breaking up the hate and bad feelings that used to be held against the Negro," black union activist Jim Cole explained to an interviewer in the late 1930s.[5]

The formation of industrial unions in meatpacking allowed black packinghouse workers to do more than simply play a central role in their neighborhoods. Through the CIO-affiliated United Packinghouse Workers of America (UPWA), they transformed the working conditions and living standards of all packinghouse workers. Chicagoan Todd Tate's recollections capture the material accomplishments of the UPWA. He recalled that in the preunion days of the 1930s, packinghouse workers "used to have run-down shoes and beat-up old jalopies." By the 1950s, he explained, "you're driving a Cadillac, wearing a suit and tie." The upward mobility imparted by the UPWA's material successes in collective bargaining made black packinghouse workers part of America's blue-collar middle class.[6]

The UPWA also served as a vehicle for the advancement of the racial concerns of black packinghouse workers and contributed significantly to the postwar civil rights movement. To an extent unparalleled in other unions, black packinghouse workers were able to use the structures of the UPWA to combat racial discrimination as well as economic exploitation. This involved, in the first instance, the use of direct-action tactics at work to eliminate inequities in treatment, job assignment, and promotion. Later, the grievance and seniority provisions of the union contract were used to equalize pay differentials and to attack segregation inside packing plants. Although issues of economic equality remained paramount, UPWA local unions in the postwar period forged dynamic alliances with the black community and spearheaded efforts to attack discrimination in housing and schools, protest police brutality, open up new avenues of black employment, and mobilize the black vote. Significantly, these activities occurred with at least the tacit, and often the active, support of white packinghouse workers.

The narratives of this book weave these themes together in a richness and complexity that this short introduction can only begin to convey. The next few pages place these stories in their context: within the history of the meatpacking industry and the formation of an industrial union of packinghouse workers.

Black Workers and the American Meatpacking Industry

Black workers entered meatpacking because of the labor needs of one of America's first mass production industries. Until the 1970s, Armour, Cudahy, Swift, and Wilson dominated the meatpacking industry. Collectively known as the Big Four, these companies controlled meat production in America's Midwestern heartland, from St. Paul in the north to Fort Worth in the south, stretching as far west as Denver and as far east as Detroit. These firms accounted for 78 percent of the total value of meat products sold in 1937.[7]

The expansion of the Big Four's Midwestern plants rested on their ability to significantly expand the productivity of labor so as to take advantage of an extensive distribution and sales network. Prior to 1860, local firms provided most meat in the United States because it was not possible for the perishable product to be shipped over long distances. After the Civil War, large firms began to displace local concerns by building huge processing operations in urban rail hubs that employed a detailed division of labor and economies of scale to reduce production costs.

The introduction of refrigeration facilitated this reorganization of meat production by allowing meat to be processed in summer months and to be shipped longer distances. Swift was the first firm to use refrigerated railroad cars to convey meat processed in Midwestern plants to eastern population centers. Armour and other companies quickly followed Swift's lead, and firms that did not follow the same business strategy either were acquired by the large companies or restricted their trade to local markets. In the 1920s, the growth of a highway network allowed new firms located away from major urban areas to grow, including businesses such as Rath & Co. in Waterloo, Iowa. These trends slightly reduced the Big Four's dominance in the 1920s and 1930s but would alter the dynamics of the industry only after World War II.

The profits and growth of the Big Four rested on the arduous labor of men and women in this pioneering mass-production industry. From just 8,000 packinghouse workers in 1870, the number of wage earners in the booming slaughterhouses reached 70,000 by the turn of the century and 125,000 in 1925. Successive waves of immigrants entered meatpacking as their first industrial job, only to leave for more desirable employment as soon as they were able. In this manner the initial Irish and German workforce of the nineteenth century became heavily Bohemian and Eastern European by the early twentieth century. Blacks first entered the industry in Kansas City in the 1880s, but in most packing centers they worked only episodically as strikebreakers until World War I. At that time, the explosion of demand caused by the war, and the suspension of European immigration, stimulated massive recruitment of southern blacks by packing firms. By the 1920s, blacks were a significant presence in most packing centers.[8]

To take advantage of the growing demand for meat, packing firms reorganized the production process at the turn of the century. The skilled all-around butchers of the late 1800s who performed a variety of cuts on the slaughtered animal gave way in the twentieth century to knife workers and laborers with narrowly defined responsibilities. In this respect, meatpacking was similar to industries such as steel, which fragmented formerly skilled jobs into a myriad of narrow operations. However, meatpacking remained unusually labor-intensive because the irregular sizes of livestock and the peculiar angle of many butchering tasks made the introduction of machinery exceedingly difficult. "Skill has become specialized to fit the anatomy," labor economist John R. Commons observed in 1904. A study of five packing-houses in the early 1930s determined that machine operators or helpers made up only 20 percent of the workforce. Among the rest, skilled workers wielded knives and cleavers to make precise cuts in the animal carcass, and unskilled laborers hauled, carried, stuffed, or performed other operations with their hands, unaided by mechanical devices.[9]

The labor-intensive production process in meatpacking stimulated firms to rely on what industrial relations expert Summner Slichter called "the drive system" to maintain control over production. This meant, very simply, the naked use of managerial authority to make workers obey their supervisors. Until the establishment of collective bargaining, foremen generally deter-mined employment levels in their departments, controlled job assignments and layoffs, and could influence hiring decisions by recommending individu-als to the personnel office. Under a "fair" foreman, a work gang could develop and implement policies that protected each member, such as rolling layoffs at times of low production so that each employee would share time off. A harsh supervisor, though, who relied on pressure and intimidation to keep production at a high pace, could make a worker's life miserable by favoring the "good workers" over perceived troublemakers or slackers.[10]

Irregular employment and labor market segmentation compounded the harsh nature of packinghouse work. Constantly shifting production needs, reflecting the patterns of livestock availability and consumer preference, encouraged firms to keep labor costs at a minimum through frequent hiring and layoffs. Layoffs disproportionately affected new employees, who had been hired when production expanded. To retain more experienced workers, especially the skilled butchers, firms reduced their hours or shifted them into other departments rather than lay them off entirely.

The result was a workforce that resembled a horizontally layered pyramid. A small triangle at the top represented the aristocracy of highly skilled butch-ers, whose abilities made them indispensable to the packing firms. Just below this level were successive gradations of semiskilled workers who relied on relations with supervisors to avoid unemployment and remain ensconced within a firm's internal labor markets. A broad trapezoid at the bottom reflected the constantly shifting mass of temporary unskilled laborers who secured jobs for a few months, weeks, or even days at a time. For this latter group, obtaining employment required participation in the daily shape-up or "roustabout" of hundreds of men who gathered outside a packinghouse's employment office in the early morning hours. One observer of the shape-up in 1910 wrote:

> The employment agent would look over the group generally and pick out those who seemed to be the sturdiest and best fitted to do the unskilled work. So far as I could see there was no bargaining or discussion about wages, terms of employment, or anything of that sort. Just the

employment agent would tap the one he wanted on the shoulder and say, "Come along."[11]

The packing firms exploited the divisions of sex, race, and ethnicity among the packinghouse workforce to inhibit formation of labor organizations. John R. Commons recalled that during a visit to the employment offices of the Chicago Swift plant, he observed that only blond-haired, fair-skinned Nordic men had been hired that day. When queried by Commons, an employment agent candidly explained that this preference "is only for this week. Last week we employed Slovaks. We change about among different nationalities and languages. It prevents them from getting together."[12]

African Americans were the latest addition to this mixture. Although employed in meatpacking more readily than in other industries, they still faced considerable discrimination in job assignments. Elmer Thomas recalled that one never found blacks working on the "clean, easy, light" jobs. Instead they were restricted to a limited array of "nigger jobs" in the plant, which required strenuous physical exertion, exposure to unpleasant environmental conditions, and contact with the blood and gore of slaughtered animals.[13]

Inadvertently, managerial policies gave blacks an unusual degree of workplace power and the potential for upward mobility by placing many of them on the killing floors. As production cannot start in meatpacking until dead animals are available to cut and process, killing-floor workers form the most powerful department in a slaughterhouse. Moreover, the variety and complexity of killing-floor tasks created a natural internal promotional ladder. A man hired as a rough laborer could learn how to use a knife and progress to increasingly skilled tasks. Jesse Vaughn, for instance, began working as a hog driver at Roberts & Oake in 1924 soon after moving to Chicago from Alabama. At that time, racial tension and prejudice ran high, and an informal white job trust restricted black workers to low-paying, menial positions. "Them Poles wouldn't let you use no knife, not no black," he recalled. Within a few years, though, Vaughn held one of the top jobs on the kill— thanks to a sympathetic Irish foreman who taught him the necessary butchering skills during breaks. Skilled black butchers like Vaughn could earn as much or more than many black professionals in the 1930s.[14]

The unpleasant character of killing-floor work explains why such important jobs were open to blacks. As these departments provided the raw material for the entire plant, management pushed the butchers to work with a furious intensity. "Five minutes up there was like five hundred dollars," recalled an Armour plant superintendent. An inexorably moving chain from which the animals hung set the pace for the killing gangs. After workers rendered an animal unconscious and killed it, butchers cut open the carcass, removed the internal organs, and split the carcass in half before refrigerating the meat overnight. In the case of cattle, highly skilled workers known as floorsmen also separated the valuable hide from the body. A poorly placed step on the floor, slick with blood and gore, could leave a worker with a broken limb or a knife wound if he collided with another butcher. Small cuts and bruises were part of the job, as well as respiratory illnesses from the hot and steamy conditions and back injuries from constant stooping and carrying. A warm department even during the winter, killing-floor temperatures often rose to more than one hundred degrees in the summer months.[15]

A "splitter" using a large cleaver to sever a cattle carcass into two halves. This job took considerable strength and dexterity, as a poor cut could reduce the value of the meat. A task traditionally performed by black men, it was among the highest-paid jobs on the killing floors. *Photograph by Burke and Dean. Used with permission of the State Historical Society of Wisconsin [WHi (X3) 50369].*

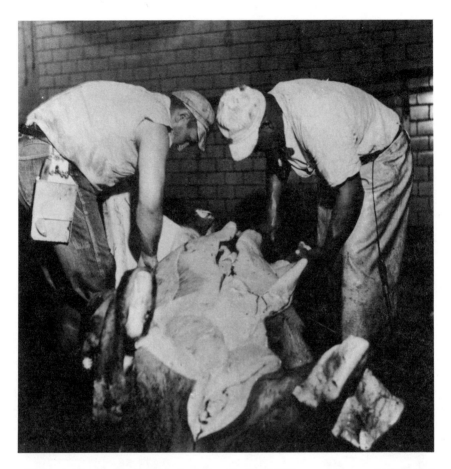

"Floorsmen" removing the hide from a cattle carcass. This was an extremely skilled job, as a nick in the hide could ruin it. Talented floorsmen often were ambidextrous. They received the highest pay rates in the entire packinghouse, equalled only by machinists and other skilled craftsmen. *Used with permission of the State Historical Society of Wisconsin [WHi (X3) 50371].*

Once the animal was dressed and chilled, the carcass was separated into component parts in the cutting rooms. White men, usually from East European ethnic groups, generally dominated these relatively clean departments. To prepare cattle for shipment to meat markets, butchers sawed the cattle halves into hind and fore quarters before hefty beef luggers carried the quarters into waiting railroad cars.

Hog carcasses received more processing. Butchers separated the carcass into hams, sides, and shoulders. Boners removed the skin and small bones from the ham and sent it down a chute to the curing cellars, where it was pickled in a brine solution. Other butchers carved specialized cuts, such as the loin and belly, and trimmed them in preparation for further processing.

Parts of the animal that could not be used for consumer cuts ended up in various by-product departments. Blood drained from slaughtered animals was collected for use in fertilizer and animal food. Cattle hides slid down a chute to the hide cellar, a "stinking place" where black men traditionally labored. Workers shook out the heavy hides, covered them with salt, and let them cure in huge piles for several months. Black men also were likely to work in the rendering department, where bones, inedible internal organs, spoiled meat, and other miscellaneous scraps were boiled and melted down for use as glue or fertilizer. The rendering house and the hide cellar were well known as the most unpleasant jobs in a packinghouse. Visitors found the stench unbearable, and the disagreeable odors permeated workers' skin and clothing, lingering even after they had showered. Chronic dermatological problems and respiratory illnesses were rife.

The hide cellar. The white workers are spreading the hides while the black worker sprinkles curing salt. These were undesirable and poorly paid jobs for both races. *Used with permission of the State Historical Society of Wisconsin [WHi (X3) 50376].*

Whereas men dominated the separation of the carcass into fresh meat cuts, women worked primarily in departments devoted to the preparation of processed foods. A survey by the Women's Bureau of the U.S. Department of Labor in the late 1920s found that more than four-fifths of all female packinghouse employees worked in just six departments. A majority of black women worked in the offal and casings rooms, which routed the internal organs of the carcass to other departments. White women predominated in cleaner jobs, such as bacon slicing, in which workers sliced and wrapped cured pig bellies in consumer-sized packages.[16]

The contrast between these two departments indicates why there were such ferocious struggles in the post–World War II period over the integration of bacon slicing operations. The offal and casings departments prepared organs such as intestines, bladders, and hearts—colloquially known as the "pluck"—for later use in processed meat products. Women in the offal room received the pluck from men in the killing areas, generally located one floor above, and then dispatched its components to appropriate departments. Intestines went next door to the adjacent casings room, where women cleaned and prepared intestines for use as containers in sausage making. Their hands were constantly immersed in the water used to clean animal organs and to flush the intestines of fat and partly digested food. Water mixed with animal fat and other bodily fluids created a slick surface on the floor of both departments; this combined with oppressive heat generated unhealthy, steamy working conditions. Women workers in casings typically suffered from debilitating conditions such as pneumonia, rheumatism, and arthritis.

In contrast, the bacon slicing room (referred to in the interviews as "sliced bacon") was carefully designed by management to present the most positive features of meatpacking. Some departments even had one glass wall to facilitate observation by tours. Visitors saw clean, well-lit rooms in which white women, neatly dressed in immaculate white uniforms, performed their tasks while seated comfortably at tables. Some plants even installed pipes carrying warm air to serve as footrests and to make the workers more comfortable without raising the room temperature. When asked by researcher Alma Herbst to justify the exclusion of blacks from this department, one management official explained simply that "only white hands are fit to touch the meat."[17]

Although the working conditions for black men on the killing floors paralleled, to some extent, those faced by black women in the offal and casings rooms, these jobs had a fundamentally different character. The killing floors had an internal line of promotion that could place men in relatively highly paid and secure jobs. In contrast, black women in the offal and casings rooms could not advance to better pay levels and more secure employment since other departments with female workers were restricted to whites. Thus, although women's struggles focused on gaining access to other female departments, the positions most highly sought by black men were the skilled trades jobs in the mechanical division. There they could learn valuable skills and escape the grueling pressure of the production line. Among men, the most bitter conflicts over departmental integration erupted when blacks tried to enter these mechanical trades positions.

The men and women who labored in meatpacking found their choices starkly limited by deeply rooted gender, racial, and ethnic patterns of workplace segmentation. While racial antagonism marked shop-floor relations prior to the 1930s, the integrated character of meat production served as the foundation for the interracial unionism of the 1930s, 1940s, and 1950s.

Black Workers and Unionism in the Meatpacking Industry

It was many years before the United Packinghouse Workers of America could capitalize on the potential for interracial unionism among packinghouse workers. For the first three decades of the twentieth century, fragmentation and racial conflict prevailed over attempts to unify the heterogeneous workforce. Two failed strikes, one in 1904 and the other in 1921 and 1922, reinforced working-class fragmentation and left bitter legacies of racial distrust and antagonism.

At the turn of the century, packinghouse workers formed their first national organization, the Amalgamated Meat Cutters and Butcher Workmen, a craft union affiliated with the American Federation of Labor. Although control of the Amalgamated rested firmly with skilled butchers, organizers largely succeeded in integrating unskilled immigrant workers into the union. In 1904, rebuff of workers' demands for a general wage increase set the stage for an epic nationwide confrontation between the union and the packing firms. The resulting strike was notable for the way skilled butchers and unskilled immigrant workers stood shoulder to shoulder in solidarity. Yet this unity was no match for the packing companies' determination to crush the union. They recruited large numbers of strikebreakers in each city, bringing trainloads of southern blacks directly into the stockyards. When production resumed, racial violence flared, as strikers vented their anger and frustration on the "scab race." Even though packing firms dismissed most blacks once the strike collapsed, the link between African Americans and strikebreaking was firmly established in the memories of white workers.

The packing companies held the upper hand until the outbreak of World War I shifted the balance of power in the nation's stockyards and packinghouses. The war shut off immigration from Europe at a moment when the meatpacking firms desperately needed an abundant pool of cheap labor to meet increased foreign demand. In order to keep their plants operating at full capacity, they tapped an important new source of labor: the stream of black migrants who were arriving in Midwestern cities in record numbers from the Deep South. In the short run, reliance on African American labor allowed the packing companies to increase production and reap record profits. In the long run, the turn to black labor affected more than the packers' balance sheets. It led to a dramatic recomposition of the workforce and decisively shaped organized labor's response to the wartime context.

The labor shortage and the employers' need for full production provided a promising opening for a new organizing campaign. In packinghouses across the country, restless workers engaged in sporadic, spontaneous strikes and job actions during 1915 and 1916. Conducted without the benefit of formal union leadership, these stoppages succeeded in pushing up wages and securing minor improvements in working conditions, yet the absence of overall coordination limited their effectiveness. For its part, the Amalgamated remained reluctant to enter the fray. Despite entreaties from union-minded activists, the union chose to ignore the ferment in the packinghouses. In July 1917, a group of radicals associated with the Chicago Federation of Labor seized the opportunity and persuaded the Federation to sponsor a campaign in the stockyards. Largely bypassing the Amalgamated, they created the Stockyards Labor Council (SLC), a federation of more than a dozen craft unions with jurisdiction in the meatpacking industry, and targeted the 35,000 workers laboring in Chicago's Union Stockyards.

By early 1918, the SLC had enrolled close to 90 percent of the white workers in Chicago's packinghouses. Organization of the 12,000 African Americans in the yards proved more difficult. While a large proportion of northern-born blacks responded favorably to the union appeal, little progress was made among the thousands of southern migrants working in the stockyards. The indifference (or outright hostility) of the major black churches and newspapers toward the movement, coupled with many blacks' aloofness toward the "white man's union," complicated this task. The packing companies, too, urged African Americans to give their loyalty to their employers and moved to solidify their relationships with black religious and civic organizations.

In late 1917, federal intervention boosted the SLC's fortunes. Fearing that continued unrest in meatpacking might disrupt essential production, Secretary of War Newton Baker established a mediation commission to stabilize industrial relations throughout the industry. The first round of arbitration resulted in a clear victory for the SLC. Judge Samuel Alschuler's award granted an 8-hour workday, a 48-hour week, the full dollar-a-week raise demanded by the union, and overtime provisions. This victory opened the way for vital membership gains among Chicago's previously recalcitrant black workers and spurred organizing efforts in other meatpacking centers.

Chicago was the key to the overall situation, and the loyalty of African American workers there remained indispensable to the ultimate success of the organizing drive. The SLC went out of its way to demonstrate its willingness to defend blacks as equals. Officials claimed that a disproportionate

40 percent of the Council's grievances came from African Americans. Blacks served alongside whites as stewards in many departments, and unprecedented steps were taken to bring the races together at union-sponsored meetings, picnics, and dances.

The end of the war in November 1918 and the ensuing demobilization intensified the contest for the loyalty of black workers. Peace in Europe rewrote the rules governing black employment in the nation's industrial centers. Practically overnight, the labor shortage that had opened job opportunities for black men and women became a labor surplus. Rounds of layoffs swept the packinghouses, and unemployment and uncertainty heightened racial friction. The SLC's decision to push forward with a campaign for 100 percent organization in June 1919 created an especially tense situation because most of the holdouts were black.

In July 1919, the worst race riot in American history swept Chicago. Although the riot began several miles from the stockyards, much of the violence played itself out in the vicinity of the packing plants. When order was restored after five days of bloodshed, 23 blacks and 15 whites lay dead. Hundreds of homes had been burned to the ground, most of them in the Back-of-the-Yards neighborhood, and another 500 people had suffered serious injuries. The riot extinguished any hope that black and white packinghouse workers might close ranks behind a common purpose. The orgy of violence sealed the fate of the SLC's organizing drive. Indeed, the Council collapsed soon after the riot, torn apart from within by factional fighting, leaving the union movement in meatpacking to the Amalgamated Meat Cutters.

Another labor-management confrontation was only a matter of time. For two more years, the Amalgamated and the packing companies continued to submit disputes to arbitration, but behind the scenes union membership declined rapidly while the packers were growing stronger. Then, in 1921, the packing firms withdrew from the arbitration agreement and unilaterally reduced wages. The Amalgamated responded by calling its local unions out on strike in December.

As was the case in 1904, it was the ease with which the packers secured replacement workers that doomed the walkout. While some black packinghouse workers stuck with the union, the great majority elected to remain at work. This decision was a pragmatic one, based on a careful weighing of options. Given the events of 1919 and the spotty record of the Amalgamated, the jobs offered by the packers were more valuable than any potential benefits the union hoped to provide. For other black workers without any previous connections to meatpacking, strikebreaking represented an opportunity for economic advancement. As the strike collapsed in January 1922, racial attitudes hardened. The legacy of this defeat was the most formidable obstacle that union organizers would face in the 1930s.

The 1921–1922 strike discredited the Amalgamated and allowed the packing companies to establish sophisticated welfare programs to appeal to workers disillusioned with labor organizations. Limited seniority, vacations, pensions, social activities, and employee representation plans fostered company allegiance among a significant cadre of black and white workers. As African Americans had demonstrated considerable antipathy toward labor organizations, employers relied more heavily on black labor and made special efforts to nurture a following among skilled black workers. One packinghouse executive candidly told a researcher in the late 1920s that the thousands of African Americans working in the industry provided a kind of "strike insurance" that made repetition of past conflict highly unlikely.[18]

Ironically, the victory of the packing firms in the 1920s shaped the subsequent success of packinghouse unionism. The outcome of the 1921–1922 strike proved, beyond any doubt, that black support was a precondition for successful organizing campaigns. Although many white packinghouse workers shared the prevailing racism of the era, they knew that a divided union movement stood little chance of success against the power and superior resources of the packing companies. Gertie Kamarczyk, a white veteran of the strike, recalled that "there was a feeling that we had to work together or the bosses were just gonna let us have it in the neck again." Joe Zabritski, who worked at one of the small houses in the Chicago yards, expressed similar sentiments. When unionism resurfaced in the 1930s, workers in his plant resigned themselves to including blacks in the new campaign. "They didn't come in and hug 'em and kiss 'em," he quickly admitted. "But they knew they had to be together, period. Even though some of them were anti-Negro, they still knew you had to be together to form a union and to win some of their demands." Thus, although the defeat of the Amalgamated Meat Cutters resulted in a legacy of fear and distrust, it also spelled the end of exclusionary unionism in the packing industry.[19]

In the 1930s, a coalition of packinghouse workers from different racial and ethnic groups overcame decades of division and fear to organize local unions in dozens of plants. The disintegration of welfare capitalism helped swing workers toward unionism as company benevolence evaporated under the economic pressures of the Depression. Wage cuts, reduced hours, and increased production pressures weakened the companies' hold over workers who had been loyal for the past decade. At the same time, the coming of the New Deal, especially pro-labor legislation such as the 1933 National Industrial Recovery Act and the 1935 National Labor Relations Act, created a favorable political climate for union advocates and emboldened rank-and-file workers.

The most striking features of the new upsurge in meatpacking was that in virtually all the major plants, black workers supplied the leadership behind the new unions. Unlike the African Americans who resisted union overtures in 1921 and supplied the pool of reserve labor that led to the strike's defeat, these workers were not recent migrants from the rural South unacquainted with industrial labor. Rather, these activists had been in the industry for a number of years and had slowly gained the respect and confidence of their white coworkers.

The decision of the newly formed Congress of Industrial Organizations (CIO) to initiate an organizing drive in meatpacking was an enormous boost to the diligent efforts of shop-floor union advocates. Through the CIO-affiliated Packinghouse Workers Organizing Committee (PWOC), formed in October 1937, packinghouse workers now had an organizational vehicle to unify the ethnic and racial groups within each plant and to coordinate the activities of unionists in different packing centers. In Chicago, the CIO's Steel Workers Organizing Committee (SWOC) lent enormous authority to the new PWOC. "The people in the yards waited a long time for the CIO," an Armour worker remembered. "When they began organizing in the steel towns and out in South Chicago, everybody wanted to know when the CIO was coming to the yards."[20]

The Steel Workers directly aided efforts to recruit African Americans in meatpacking by contributing one of the most important black leaders to the organizing drive, Henry (Hank) Johnson. The son of a radical unionist from west Texas, Johnson was well known in the black community. He had spent a number of years organizing for the International Workers' Order, was a founder of the National Negro Congress, and had been instrumental in the forging of interracial solidarity in the Steel Workers union. Contemporaries remembered him as a "fantastic organizer" and a "powerful speaker." A highly visible orator and Assistant National Director of the PWOC between 1937 and 1941, Johnson's role in the PWOC demonstrated to black workers that the union was committed to placing blacks at its very highest levels.[21]

Within the structure of PWOC-affiliated local unions, the glue holding the diverse membership together was cooperation at the point of production. Extensive departmental organizations, knitted together by stewards and executive boards with conscious representation from significant racial and ethnic groups, allowed the union apparatus to incorporate the diverse workforce. Common activity against company policies—ranging from pressing grievances to departmental job actions and plantwide walkouts—encouraged a growing confidence that blacks and whites would support each other in collective action. "Once you became UPWA, that's your sister, that's your brother," remembered Ercell Allen, a black Chicago union leader. "We did things together, black and white."[22]

Union demands for strict seniority, a grievance procedure, and a collective bargaining agreement appealed to workers of all races. Union organizers reminded blacks of past discrimination and argued that the union had the capacity and the will to curtail racist management practices. "They knew if they ever got seniority, then they wouldn't be getting laid off like they were," observed James C. Harris, a black founder of the Omaha Swift union.[23]

Many of the initial union protests over shop-floor conditions sprang from specific grievances of black workers. The best-known example concerns the

Chicago Armour local's successful effort to force the removal of stars from the time cards of blacks. For many years this practice had allowed department supervisors to single out blacks for layoffs when reducing the number of employees in a particular department. After Charles Perry, a black worker and union activist on the hog kill, was laid off despite his high seniority, simultaneous stoppages on the hog, beef, and sheep kills brought the practice of tagging time cards to a halt and won widespread support among black workers.

The Chicago incident was not unusual. Strikes by majority white plants in several cities to halt discriminatory treatment of blacks, including a 1938 plant occupation in Kansas City, showed African Americans that "we were going to be a union who would absolutely not tolerate prejudiced tendencies, no prejudicial actions whatsoever." To whites, union organizers pointed out the greater benefits they would receive through collective action, rather than reliance on individual relationships with management. "These people will protect you, if you protect them," white union leader Darrel Poe would explain to white workers at Cudahy's Omaha plant. "It takes all of us together or we're not going to go anyplace." Whites tended to back the use of union power to combat discrimination—not necessarily out of a commitment to black rights, but because racial grievances were articulated through the union in the traditional terms of job rights. Reciprocity was a factor in white support as well, since in numerous instances the predominantly black killing floors shut down to support the demands of white workers in other departments.[24]

Political leftists played an important role in this process of building an alliance between white and black workers. Their impact was especially pronounced in Chicago, where the Communist Party had a highly organized presence at the Armour plant, and influence inside other facilities in the stockyards. Elsewhere, individual white leftists such as Charles R. Fischer in Kansas City and Punchy "CIO" Ackerson in Waterloo also were prominent advocates of cooperation among workers without regard to race. Their positive role induced black militant Sam Parks to credit the "left whites and Communist whites" with making a "hell of a difference" in the UPWA because of the example they set "cooperating and working with blacks." The ideological commitment of leftists to interracial unity helped to accentuate this tendency in the nascent unions of the Depression decade.

Union organizers' appeals for interracial industrial unionism in the 1930s were successful. In 1943, when delegates from hundreds of meatpacking local unions formed the United Packinghouse Workers of America, blacks were visible in leadership positions throughout the new International union. In addition to their role at the local level, blacks held the vice presidency of the UPWA, seats on the International Executive Board, and important staff positions. The new union's constitution explicitly stated its commitment to an interracial organization, and its contracts prohibited discrimination on the basis of race.

World War II enhanced black influence in the UPWA. As whites fled meatpacking for better jobs in booming defense industries, blacks took their places. There, the willingness of local UPWA officials and shop stewards to engage in job actions, despite the no-strike pledge of the International union, trained migrants new to industrial conditions in the UPWA's brand of militant unionism. Increasingly, these new black workers included World War II veterans who had fought under segregated conditions and were no longer willing to abide by the patterns of racial deference that their parents' generation had tolerated. "Guys came out of the military and they didn't give a damn about the Ku Klux Klan," recalled one black union leader. "You had a breed of people who said, 'Hell, I'm entitled to this—I want it!'"25

Black commitment to unionism, in an alliance with whites, gave the UPWA considerable industrial power. By the end of the war, pattern bargaining was solidly entrenched in meatpacking through national master agreements with the major packing companies. To exert power within the multiplant Big Four firms, workers created "chains" of local unions in different plants of the same national concern. These chains met regularly to set bargaining objectives and, if necessary, to coordinate strikes and slowdowns designed to reduce employer resistance to the union's demands. The master agreements standardized wages and working conditions throughout the meatpacking industry, as scores of individual contracts with smaller firms automatically set their wages at the level of the large firms.

A new round of conflict with the packing companies in the years immediately after the war threatened to unravel the UPWA's accomplishments. A short strike in 1946 (settled only through the intervention of the federal government) was followed two years later by a brutal confrontation that began in March 1948 and lasted for two months. The main issue was wages: the packing firms offered a 9-cent-per-hour increase and the UPWA stuck to its demand for 29 cents, even after the rival Amalgamated Meat Cutters accepted the companies' offer.

Much as they had after World War I, packing firms tried to undermine the 1948 strike by bringing strikebreakers into their facilities. In response, the union relied on mass picket lines to block access to the plants, even when hindered by court injunctions. The daily confrontations occasionally erupted into violent clashes. Chicago unionists contended with a force of one thousand police who used squads of club-wielding officers to escort strikebreakers through picket lines. In late April, Chicago UPWA member Santo Cicardo was killed by a truck that police allowed to speed toward a union picket line. In Kansas City, a police riot wrecked the Cudahy local's union hall.

17

UPWA leaders marching in the Chicago funeral procession for Santo Cicardo. From left to right: UPWA Vice President Philip Weightman, UPWA President Ralph Helstein, District One Director Herbert March, Secretary-Treasurer Lewis J. Clark, and Chicago Armour Local 347 President Sam Curry. *Photo courtesy of Herbert March.*

The largest clashes of the strike erupted in early May, after the companies mobilized an aggressive back-to-work movement. Hundreds, and sometimes thousands, of strike supporters confronted strikebreakers in dozens of cities. In St. Paul, union members defied a court injunction and blockaded the main entrance to the stockyards. Pickets repulsed several police charges, overturned cars, and used their fists to disperse scabs. A riot erupted in Waterloo, Iowa, after black strikebreaker Fred Lee Roberts fatally shot white union member Chuck Farrell in front of Rath & Co.'s front gate. Within a few days, however, the use of police, court injunctions, and the National Guard in several places prevented union pickets from halting the entry of strikebreakers into the plants. With many packinghouses steadily increasing their operations, the union called off the strike, accepted the companies' nine-cent-per-hour wage increase offer, and returned to work on May 19.

The UPWA's expanded anti-discrimination program was forged in the difficult aftermath of the 1948 strike. The bruised union returned to work in early May on the packers' terms, with hundreds of local leaders discharged and the International unable to pay staff salaries. Membership declined from one hundred thousand at the beginning of the strike to around sixty thousand just after its conclusion. Despite these problems, there was no apparent increase in racial tensions among UPWA members. Throughout the strike, "blacks and whites were just like two black-eyed peas," recalled Fort Worth black union leader Eddie Humphrey. "We were all in the same pod. We were all after the same thing." A 1949 survey showed that 96 percent of the UPWA locals felt that black strike participation was as good as, or better than, the activity of whites.[26]

In contrast to the 1921–1922 national meatpacking strike, which drove deep fissures between black and white workers, the 1948 strike enhanced black power in the UPWA and accelerated the union's commitment to civil rights. The picket line clashes and economic hardship experienced by all strikers reinforced the bonds between workers of different races and ethnicity and instilled the UPWA's militancy in a new generation of union activists. "They fell right in cycle," recalled Waterloo leader Charles Pearson. The "generation of '48" (as they were known) learned "that we have to fight for ours, too, if we're going to keep it." In addition, the high level of union organization during the strike drew new groups of workers, often black, into union activity. With the loss of many secondary leaders, the UPWA drew new committed union members into positions as stewards and local union officials.[27]

In an effort to hold the union together in the wake of the 1948 strike, UPWA president Ralph Helstein asked John Hope II of Fisk University to conduct a race relations survey of the organization. Helstein's motivation was straightforward: "I felt there had to be something affirmative going on outside of an area in which the companies could screw us." The surveys graphically depicted the extent and limits of the UPWA's interracial coalition. On the positive side, they confirmed high levels of black union participation: blacks were stewards in 83 percent of UPWA locals and held executive board positions in 73 percent.

However, the surveys also revealed alarming signs of racial prejudice and job segregation in UPWA-organized packinghouses. More than 30 percent of white members objected to working with a black in the same job classification, and 90 percent of southern whites supported segregated eating facilities. Whites filled 96 percent of the Department of Labor's 44 meatpacking job categories, whereas blacks were present in only 54 percent. In many cases, blacks and whites dressed in separate locker rooms; in the South, they used separate drinking fountains, rest rooms, and other facilities in accordance with prevalent Jim Crow laws and customs.[28]

On the basis of these findings, the UPWA's 1950 convention adopted a comprehensive anti-discrimination program and established an Anti-Discrimination Department, headed by black International Vice President Russell Lasley. Local unions received detailed instructions on the formation of anti-discrimination committees and were encouraged to confront patterns of segregation inside packinghouses, hiring discrimination, and community racism. The union also made a significant decision to alter and strictly enforce a nondiscrimination clause that had appeared in all UPWA contracts since 1941. Instead of simply prohibiting discrimination against employees, the International demanded that the packing firms add the word "applicant." Potentially, this gave the union the power to halt discrimination against blacks in the employment office.[29]

While the international union apparatus provided a lever for anti-discrimination activity, the independent initiatives of local unions determined the extent to which the UPWA's programs were actually implemented. "It was up to the local people to say, this is what's hurting me here," explained Anna Mae Weems, a dynamic black leader of Waterloo's packinghouse workers. In this respect, the application of the union's expanded anti-discrimination program was consistent with, relied on, and reinforced the shop-floor structure and rank-and-file orientation of the UPWA. Moreover, in locals with a white majority, international policies provided considerable leverage for black activists to utilize the union apparatus for civil rights activity.[30]

If the International's programs provided the lever, Chicago packinghouse locals were the fulcrum for expanded civil rights activity by local unions elsewhere. The black majority unions at the huge Armour, Swift, and Wilson plants, employing more than ten thousand workers, were the keystone to the UPWA's industrial power. While white UPWA members probably recoiled from the aggressive "supermilitancy" of leading black activists and the openly Communist views of top officials such as District Director Herbert March, the union's ability to secure national contracts unquestionably rested on the strength and vitality of the Chicago locals. By engaging in a wide range of anti-discrimination activities, the Chicago unions encouraged civil rights initiatives in other cities.

There were three broad areas to the UPWA's expanded anti-discrimination activity. First, unionists identified discriminatory practices in their own plants and tried to correct them. This included integrating segregated departments, dressing rooms, and other plant facilities, and ending hiring discrimination against black women. Second, locals attacked discriminatory practices in their communities, primarily restrictions on black access to bars, restaurants, and public facilities, as well as employment barriers by local businesses. Finally, packinghouse workers consciously worked with and influenced community-based organizations, especially local branches of the NAACP (the National Association for the Advancement of Colored People).

Within the plants, local unions began a concerted campaign to integrate all-white departments. Local Anti-Discrimination Committees encouraged black workers to use their seniority to transfer into these areas, and they prepared for potential problems by arranging departmental meetings with whites and informing management of union intentions. Local union officials who supported these efforts would inform reluctant white workers "either work with them or you find another job," recalled Kansas City Armour steward Nevada Isom. "That was spelled out to them and they cooperated very nicely." Union victories were impressive: within five years black men and women broke through historic racial barriers in dozens of plants from California to New Jersey and from Fort Worth to St. Paul.[31]

Closely linked with departmental integration were union efforts to use the "applicant" contract clause to end hiring discrimination against black women. Chicago unions were the first to utilize this contractual provision to attack employment inequities. In 1950, the Swift local arranged for both black and white women to apply for jobs and carefully monitored the company's response to the applicants. While Swift officials courteously ushered white women into its offices, interviewed them, and then hired them, they brusquely turned black women away with the excuse that there were no openings. The local filed a grievance against Swift and won a landmark ruling requiring the company to hire the black women with back pay from the date they had initially applied. Over the next few years, dozens of plants followed Chicago Swift's example, leading to the hiring of black women by all major packing companies, as well as smaller plants and other food-processing operations.

The campaigns of UPWA locals against discrimination in the packinghouses encouraged an impressive level of community-based civil rights activity. Union members targeted problems that had long angered blacks and remained prevalent in the 1950s: housing segregation, refusal of businesses to serve or employ blacks, and restrictions against black access to schools and recreational facilities. These community-oriented efforts by UPWA members spilled over to and influenced other civil rights groups, especially the NAACP. Union aggressiveness intersected with the efforts of NAACP Labor Secretary Herbert Hill to expand the trade union base of the predominantly middle-class organization. "When we got active, the NAACP was called a 'tea sipping' organization—silk-stocking," reflected Todd Tate. With the cooperation of international UPWA leaders, local union stewards in plants across the country recruited thousands of black and white UPWA members to the NAACP in the 1950s. In some areas, packinghouse workers transformed local chapters previously dominated by black professionals and drew them into the union's civil rights activity.[32]

The bulk of these activities took place before the 1955–1956 Montgomery Bus Boycott catapulted a young minister, the Reverend Martin Luther King Jr., into national prominence. The UPWA immediately rallied to support the boycott and developed a firm alliance with King that lasted until his death. The UPWA brought King to its 1957 Anti-Discrimination Conference and

UPWA delegates at 1957 NAACP convention with Herbert Hill. From left to right: Field Representative Ollie Webb, Local 117 Chief Steward Richard Miller, District One Director Charles Hayes, Field Representative Addie Wyatt, Herbert Hill, AFL-CIO Representative Philip Weightman, UPWA Vice President Russell Lasley. *Photograph by Edward Bailey. Used with permission of the State Historical Society of Wisconsin [WHi (X3) 50370].*

presented him with an $11,000 check—amassed entirely through local union donations—to fund a voter registration project by the newly formed Southern Christian Leadership Conference (SCLC).

The Packinghouse Workers' support for King's activities continued throughout the late 1950s and 1960s. The UPWA was one of the few unions to assist King's organizing efforts in Chicago in 1966 and to side with him in 1967 when King spoke out against U.S. involvement in the Vietnam War.

The UPWA's participation in the national civil rights movement was not limited to support for King and the NAACP. The union developed a close relationship with the Highlander Folk School, backed James Foreman's work, and mobilized in defense of sharecroppers evicted from their fields by landlords in 1959 for having the temerity to try to register to vote. It also endorsed the lunch-counter sit-ins organized by the Student Non-Violent

Coordinating Committee (SNCC) in 1960 and 1961 and placed union pickets at northern franchises of stores targeted by the SNCC.

But just as the civil rights movement was accelerating in the late 1950s and early 1960s, the UPWA was forced into a rearguard battle against the

Martin Luther King Jr. receiving an $11,000 check from UPWA Vice President Russell Lasley to fund voter registration efforts in the South. The presentation took place at the union's 1957 Anti-Discrimination Conference. UPWA President Ralph Helstein is on the right. *Used with permission of the State Historical Society of Wisconsin [WHi (X3) 50373].*

UPWA picket at a Des Moines Woolworth Store, 1960. *Used with permission of the State Historical Society of Wisconsin [WHi (X3) 50378].*

biggest threat it could face: the closure of unionized packing plants. Beginning with the Chicago stockyards, dozens of packinghouses in the old urban meatpacking hubs shut their doors. Between 1956 and 1965, Armour closed 21 major plants employing more than 14,000 workers, including its facilities in Chicago, Fort Worth, and Kansas City. American UPWA membership fell to 70,000 by 1967 from a high of 103,600 in 1953. As these old, multistory packinghouses shut down, they were replaced by smaller single-story facilities located in the countryside near the source of livestock. As a result, the number of packinghouse workers in urban areas fell by more than 50,000 between 1963 and 1984, and the proportion of workers in rural plants increased from 25 percent to 50 percent of the national workforce.[33]

Rapid technological change also decreased employment in meatpacking, especially among women workers. Food processing departments proved far easier to automate than the fresh meat areas, and with the increasing consumer demand for these products after World War II, meatpacking firms had ample motivation to increase productivity. Circular electric "wizard" knives in the offal and trim departments reduced the workforce by doubling productivity. In the bacon department, new slicing and weighing machines reduced labor needs by 40 to 60 percent. Technological innovation also disrupted well-established boundaries between male and female jobs, inciting intense gender conflicts in many local unions.

The changes in workforce composition had profound effects on the UPWA as the base for dynamic social unionism dwindled. Preoccupied with plant closings and technological change, its activist base eroding, the UPWA was placed on the defensive. While retaining its unusually progressive stands, aggressive "outreach" programs collapsed in the 1960s "because there was no one to carry them on."[34]

The changing terrain of meat production disproportionately affected black workers. Work in meatpacking no longer could provide "the strength of the black community" as it had between 1914 and 1960. The abrupt closure of this traditional avenue of employment and occupational advancement dealt a severe blow to urban black communities experiencing a new wave of migration from the South. No longer would migrants head north with the objective of obtaining work in meatpacking.

Conclusion

In his speech to the UPWA's 1957 Anti-Discrimination Conference, Martin Luther King captured the hope of that gathering when he predicted, "Organized labor can be one of the most powerful instruments to do away with this evil that confronts our nation that we refer to as segregation and discrimination. It is certainly true that the forces that are anti-Negro are by and large anti-labor, and with the coming together of the powerful influence of labor and all people of good will in the struggle for freedom and human dignity, I can assure you that we have a powerful instrument." King's hope for an alliance with the labor movement was inspired by the manner in which the UPWA, an interracial (and majority white) organization, was able to improve both the living standards and civil rights of black packinghouse workers.[35]

The black experience in meatpacking, and within the UPWA, is a positive story with important lessons for today. It shows how access to well-paying jobs was a source of pride and upward mobility for two generations of black men and women and a source of stability for many Midwestern black communities. It indicates how a democratic union could tap the abilities of blacks who had prior organizational experience and could provide opportunities for other African Americans to learn organizational skills that could be put to good use elsewhere. It also demonstrates how an alliance between working-class whites and blacks worked to the benefit of both groups.

25

Several distinctive features of the American meatpacking industry fostered these outcomes. The most important was the substantial presence of black workers in key jobs, which made it impossible for unions and company management to ignore the issue of race and made it more likely that unionization would work to the benefit of African Americans, since forming a viable labor organization without them was not possible.

Still, these favorable conditions do not sufficiently explain the dramatic expansion of the UPWA's civil rights program after World War II. Two additional factors are critical here: the militancy of black workers who pushed the union to take greater steps against racial discrimination, and the support for these programs by white workers. Although only a small minority of whites actually participated in the union's civil rights initiatives, a majority of them needed to tolerate these activities in order for them to occur. "I'm not going to say we broke down the social barriers which they had," admitted UPWA president Ralph Helstein. "But there is no doubt that in terms of the union itself there was a lot of change that took place." The limits to the changes in racial attitudes of white members, accurately summarized by Helstein, should not negate the UPWA's important accomplishment. With the strong encouragement of their union, working-class whites could be brought to support the efforts of blacks to end racial discrimination.[36]

The UPWA's record on civil rights made it an unusual union in postwar America. Unlike most unions affiliated with the AFL-CIO, it remained a democratic organization responsive to its members. The ability of black packinghouse workers to use the UPWA to achieve upward mobility and racial equality indicates how internal democracy was an important asset to the union's bargaining power and its pursuit of a better society for working people of all races. It is unfortunate that more American unions did not emulate the UPWA.

This story is certainly relevant today. The narratives in this book show that there is no substitute for good, stable jobs if we are to see improvement in the living standards of the African American community and a decline in racial tension. Although few would disagree with this basic point, the vehicle through which the black workers in this book improved themselves will arouse more controversy in today's political climate. Central to black advancement in meatpacking was their ability to use an interracial organization constituted along class lines—a labor union—which employed confrontational tactics against employers and uncooperative political officials. The role of employment in meatpacking as an avenue for black upward mobility came about through the initiatives of black workers themselves, and were given focus and power through the vehicle of a trade union. In a society where progress for African Americans is extremely difficult, we need to listen closely to, and learn from, the experiences, stories, and opinions of these black packinghouse workers.

2

"WE MADE A RELIGION OF UNITY"
Black and White Workers
in Chicago's Packinghouses

The development of Chicago's black community in the twentieth century was intertwined closely with the city's packinghouses. Located a few miles southwest of the downtown Loop, the Union Stockyards complex formed one of America's largest industrial concentrations and was the center of the nation's meatpacking industry. In addition to operating major plants there, Armour, Wilson, and Swift headquartered their operations in the Windy City. A host of smaller independent packers—including P. D. Brennan, Roberts & Oake, Miller & Hart, Agar, Reliable, and Illinois Meat—clustered in the shadows of the giant packinghouses. At its peak, more than 40,000 men and women labored in the enormous slaughterhouses, sprawling livestock pens, fertilizer plants, and soap works clustered in this single square mile. Polish, Irish, Lithuanian, and Slavic workers from the adjacent Back-of-the-Yards neighborhood and African American workers living in the city's Black Belt, a mile and a quarter to the east, entered the yards each day and helped make Chicago, in poet Carl Sandburg's words, "hog butcher for the world."

African American workers labored in Chicago's packinghouses as early as the 1890s, but their numbers were negligible. Although the packers relied heavily on black labor to undermine the strike of 1904, they dismissed most of these workers once the union capitulated. It was not until World War I that black workers constituted a large and permanent component of the workforce. With immigration from war-torn Europe virtually halted, and with orders for meat products at an all-time high, the packers turned to black migrants from the South to keep their plants operating at full capacity.

Between 50,000 and 70,000 black southerners relocated to Chicago during the Great Migration, which occurred during and immediately after the First World War. Pushed out of the South by crop failures and an upsurge in racist violence, and drawn north by the lure of industrial employment, these migrants more than doubled the size of Chicago's black community and helped make the city's Southside Black Belt an African American city within a city—a ghetto suffering from overcrowding, crime, and dilapidated housing, but at the same time a vital center of black culture and politics rivaled only by New York's Harlem.

Meatpacking was a crucial part of the economic life of this ghetto, or "Bronzeville," as it was known. By the war's end, the proportion of black workers in the packinghouses had climbed from 3 percent to 25 percent. In the large plants, African Americans accounted for more than 30 percent of the labor force. Indeed, the meatpacking industry emerged at this time as the single most important source of employment for blacks in Chicago. At the end of the decade, one out of every two black men who held jobs in manufacturing was employed in the stockyards.

Unlike the black workers who found jobs in steel and other area industries, black packinghouse workers were not restricted to the least-skilled and most menial positions. Largely due to the packers' desire to undermine white labor organization, black workers increasingly performed skilled "knife jobs" on the killing floors and in the cutting departments. African Americans who held these coveted positions received wages that placed them near the top of the black community's class structure. Lowell Washington, whose father moved to Chicago from Mississippi, explained that

> My dad worked hard, but because of it we were pretty well off—to be a top man at Swifts or Armours meant that you could pay your bills, feed your family, have your kids in clothes and shoes, and have more than a little bit of respect from your neighbors. For a working man, and I mean a black working man, you could hope to be one of those Pullman porters, but the next best thing was to earn top dollar over in a packinghouse, and even if you were just a 16-year-old kid shoveling shit out in the yards, you knew that you could get inside one of those plants, and then you could learn a skill and make some real money.[1]

The presence of black workers in Chicago's packinghouses, and their advancement into skilled jobs, presented a challenge to organized labor. For a brief period during the war it seemed that the new style of inclusive unionism practiced by the Stockyards Labor Council (SLC) might bridge the gulf between immigrant and African American workers, but the 1919 race riot dashed these hopes. Racial friction intensified afterward and, in part, contributed to the demise of the SLC. A strike in 1921 failed when black packinghouse workers opted to remain at work rather than cast their lot with Amalgamated Meat Cutters.

During the 1920s, Chicago's packinghouses were nonunion citadels. Divided by cleavages of race and ethnicity, wooed by the packers' ambitious program of welfare capitalism, and living in fear of the blacklist and company spies, workers dared not risk open organization. It required the shock of the Depression and the optimism of the New Deal to create new opportunities for union advocates. Significantly, when packinghouse unionism resurfaced in the 1930s, black workers stood at the center of the movement. Unlike the migrants of the 1910s, these were seasoned veterans of the yards who shared the work-related grievances of other workers and were able to provide powerful leadership by virtue of their strategic positions on the animal killing floors.

From the moment the CIO chartered the Packinghouse Workers Organizing Committee (PWOC) in 1937, the Chicago stockyards formed the focus of the union campaign. Although organization progressed most rapidly in the small houses of the "Little Six" independent plants, it was the PWOC's 1939 victory in Armour's Chicago plant that allowed the union to establish itself in the industry. Contracts with Swift and Wilson soon followed, although all three big packers stubbornly resisted the shop-floor power of the union throughout the war years.

When the United Packinghouse Workers of America was established in 1943, Chicago remained the headquarters of the International union. The large Chicago locals—Armour 347, Swift 28, and Wilson 25—acted as leaders in their respective chains, and many key staff members were recruited from the ranks of the Chicago membership.

Demographic trends evidenced in the other packing centers were felt more keenly in Chicago. Especially important was the racial recomposition of the workforce that began during the Second World War and continued apace through the 1950s. While black workers continued to enter the packinghouses, many whites exited for cleaner and lighter jobs first in the burgeoning defense sector and later in construction and metal manufacturing. At the time of the UPWA's 1948 strike, approximately half the Chicago membership was African American. When the packinghouses began to close in the late 1950s, nearly three-quarters of the workforce was black.

The weight of numbers, coupled with a tradition of militant egalitarianism, made Chicago the center of civil rights activity in the UPWA. In addition to breaking down discriminatory practices within the packinghouses, Chicago locals pushed their "A-D" campaign beyond the confines of the yards into the larger community. Here, they joined with established groups such as the NAACP and the Urban League, as well as with a number of ad hoc organizations, to combat segregation, mob violence, and other problems that plagued African Americans in the city.

Although plant closures had eroded the social base for activism within the UPWA by the time that Martin Luther King brought his movement to Chicago in 1966, packinghouse leaders played important roles in the struggle for open housing and formed a crucial bridge between organized labor and civil rights activists. While this was the UPWA's last crusade, individual packinghouse activists carried their commitments and orientation into other unions and other organizations.

Philip Weightman

Philip Weightman was born in 1902 in Vicksburg, Mississippi. His father—a skilled craftsman who worked as a butcher, brickmaker, and bricklayer—moved the family north to St. Louis in 1917. Here, father and son worked together at a number of jobs before entering the Armour plant across the river in East St. Louis. Philip remained at Armour until 1920, working on the hog kill. For a brief period, he was involved in the organizing campaign conducted by the Amalgamated Meat Cutters. Between 1920 and 1926, he worked as a butcher at Swift Dressed Beef, a subsidiary of Swift and Company, and for three years after that he labored at the Krey Packing Company. In 1929, Weightman left St. Louis and moved to Chicago, where he again worked briefly at Armour before moving over to the Swift plant.

A sports enthusiast, Weightman worked with the company to organize a baseball league among its employees. In the late 1930s, the PWOC organization in the plant recruited Weightman, who had been a loyal "company man" since his ill-fated encounter with the Amalgamated nearly 20 years earlier. He quickly emerged as one of the Local 28's key leaders; coworkers elected him local union president in 1939. He was one of the more prominent black unionists in Chicago and throughout the packing industry at this time. When the UPWA was founded in 1943, Weightman became its International vice president and also served as head of the Grievance Department.

Weightman's recollections about his father and early childhood provide a fascinating glimpse into the life and world of black craftsmen in the early twentieth-century South. His multistep migration to Chicago, employment in meatpacking, and acquisition of butchering skills epitomize the experience of hundreds of other African American packinghouse workers.

My father was a jack-of-all-trades. He loved butchering; he made brick; he laid brick; he excavated buildings. My father told me about making brick in a brick kiln, that he could make more brick per hour. He was a fast guy in all the work that he did. He could make and lay more brick in that time than the average bricklayer could.

My father was a half-breed; he had a white father, but my grandmother was a part of a group of sisters that was reared in Brunswick, Virginia, and during the slavery time they migrated to Vicksburg, and the slave owners refused to break up that family of girls. My father was a first cousin to a white family by the name of Hall. Frank Hall was a butcher who had a meat market separated from the grocery store; it was purely a meat market. And naturally, my father being a half-breed and sort of cousin in that family, he got some advantages that some of the other blacks didn't get. My father was a meat market butcher as well as a slaughterhouse butcher.

I remember as a kid following my father to a pasture, where out in that pasture was a number of head of cattle. And off from this one-room building

Philip Weightman, standing in front on the right, at a lunchtime rally in front of the Chicago Swift plant, about 1941. *Used with permission of the State Historical Society of Wisconsin [WHi (X3) 50379].*

there was a small lot. They would drive a number of head of cattle into that lot, and they would select the bullock that they were going to slaughter that day. They had what was known as a bull ring: it was a round metal ring in the center of the floor. They would put a rope through that bull ring and loop it over the head of that cattle they were going to slaughter, and pull them into that bull ring. They had a big post off to the side, and while they were pulling, they wrapped the rope around it. Then they would knock the animal to stun it and then proceed to kill it. I was the salt boy. Once the animal was skinned, I sprinkled the salt over it. Slipping and sliding, bust my behind! And it was a lot of fun. I think that it was from that I got the instinct for liking to butcher.

In Vicksburg I went to St. Mary's Catholic through the fourth or fifth grade, and then I got a job. You know, poverty-stricken family and all that, all these kids my father had, four of us at home, two gone and got married. I went to work for the Burke Construction Company, and I never did make it back to school. But do you know what I did? I developed a habit. I would listen to people talk about books. I went to the library. That clerk in the library learned to recognize me. I would come in, and she always had a stack of books for me. I was sort of graded by people who were teachers, said I was ready for high school. And do you know, I took high school at night, a summer's high school in Vicksburg. Summer. And I didn't ever graduate, but I was given credit for the eleventh grade. And it was satisfying. I took all kinds of courses, everything I could think of, every book I could read.

Anyway, I got a job with the Burke Construction Company. They were building a big brick building, and I got a job there as a water boy. I always loved the plastering—how a guy could show off with the plaster. Oh, I thought that was beautiful. Back in those days, who were the plasterers? They were all black. The bricklayers? All black. They were artists, real artists. On this job there were no white bricklayer, no white plasterer anywhere around. But there was no union. And back in that day, I drove a hitch team, building the waterworks in Vicksburg—a pair of horses pulling up the load of dirt out of a hole.

My father had left Vicksburg to go up North in 1916. He stopped on the way in Memphis at my sister's house, and from there he went on to St. Louis, and finally my mother left to be with him. I was the oldest boy, and then there was my next brother Charlie, and sister Frances, and a young baby brother, Philander; they were sort of under my keep. We finally got a train, went to Memphis, and stayed there a while, and finally we went on to St. Louis and established home in October of 1917.

We went to work at the American Car and Foundry Company, and that's where my father made me a man. It was paying twenty-seven and a half cents an hour, and Father got a job and got me a job there, too. He had to swear that I was one year older than what I was. I was the sawdust boy—watched the sawdust coming from the planing mill to the furnace, seeing that it didn't get blocked on the way. And I got seventeen and a half cents an hour. Come the summertime we went to sleep up there, almost covered up with sawdust! [laughing] Oh boy!

My father got a contract to unload coal into the boiler room, through the winter. It was mostly slag and one-inch nuts. And we got a contract for that fifty-ton car, and this is where my father made me a man. That car would pull up there, and there were two windows, one at this end, one at that end. My father said, "Phil, we can get a contract here to unload coal; we get ten dollars a car. Do you think you can help me?" And so he said, "OK, let's try it this way. You take this end of the car and I'm going to take that end." I was a stubborn young guy, and I said to myself, "When Pop gets to the center of that car, I'm going to be there, too." And damn it to hell, when he got to the center of the car, I was there! We unloaded two of those cars a day, twelve hours a day, but we unloaded two of them.

Finally the cold weather caught up with us. Shoveling outdoors there, we couldn't take that winter, being southern. [laughs] And Pop said, "Let's go and see if we can't get a job back in a packinghouse." We went to Swift and

Company, and Swift hired Pop right away. Pop said, "I've got a son here, hire him." They said, "We don't want your son, we want you." He said, "Well if you can't hire my son, you can't have me." That's how close we were together. So we left there and went down to Armour and Company, and they hired both of us. They sent me to the hog kill department and sent him to the cooler area, where the meat first goes in to cool before it's put into the freezer. So that was my beginning in the packinghouse work. We worked there, and finally Pop got laid off, and they wanted to keep me, and he then says that I stay. I can understand why: I would be the breadwinner till he could do something.

Just before Weightman's family arrived in St. Louis, one of the worst race riots in American history raged just across the Mississippi River in East St. Louis. Sparked by local manufacturers' attempts to drive down wages through the use of black labor, the riot erupted after a shooting incident near an aluminum plant. White mobs attacked the black community, burning a large portion of it to the ground and rendering six thousand homeless. At the end of two days of violence, at least 40 blacks and 9 whites had been killed.

Everything was squeamish when we got there. Out on Broadway there, that's where the blacks were burnt up in their homes. The rioters didn't let them out. There's never been a count on how many were burnt; an awful lot were burnt, burnt their houses up with the people in them. The blacks in St. Louis were attempting to go to their rescue, armed, but they put a blockade at the bridges so they couldn't get across and they couldn't swim the river. There was a lot of people killed. It never was reported, the number, really. Hundreds of people, children, burnt up in that fire. There was a lot of bitterness, a lot of bitterness.

I left Armour in 1920 and went to work for Swift Dressed Beef and worked at the Swift plant till 1926. And there my unionism began. We had no union, not even a company union at that plant, but we were having problems, conflict with management, and I became their leader.

We would go to fabricate in the morning and slaughter in the afternoon—cutting up the meat, making the loins and pork chops and everything like that in the morning, and then in the afternoon we slaughtered. There was an influx of Polish workers and black workers. We had a close working relationship—strange as it might seem—a togetherness. Blacks and whites were exploited in the packing industry for many, many years, but there was an innate feeling towards one another and support of one another. Polish workers at that time weren't resentful of blacks.

There was a band saw; you sawed the butts off from the picnic hams. That's a band saw, and you know how fast they run. And when that saw happens to break, it scoots off. Vroom! If it hit anybody, it would cut 'em half in two. It had no safety on that thing, nothing. Well, I'm right next to there, boning shoulders, that's taking the neck bone out of the shoulder before that shoulder was pushed to that guy to saw it. I kept saying to the guy next to me, "Isn't there some way that we can do something about that? Suppose that damn saw breaks, and instead of going that way comes over here? We're dead!" So the three of us went to the foreman and said, "Look, is there some way, somehow, you could put something round this thing?" "No. That's the way the company give it to us; that's the way you have to work on it. If you don't want to work on it, you don't work; we'll find somebody else and put 'em there. It's up to you." Oh God! So I swallowed hard on that. For a year didn't do nothing about it. Finally a guy gets his fingers sawn off.

Then there's what is known as a belly bench. They have to trim this bacon in a perfect trim, according to standard regulations, for it to cure and then smoke. Well, that's hard work. So the guys say, "What are we going to do about this? We don't have enough people." Again I was the spokesman, went to the foreman, a young guy who used to be a worker, and said, "You know what this is all about. Why in hell don't you do something? Give us some more help. Because if you don't, somebody's going to get cut, cut seriously. And then what happens? The company's got a bill on their hands." He said, "You've been doing it all the time, you're going to continue." Our men had an hour for lunch. We came back and walked up to him as a unit and said, "You put somebody else on there, or we don't work no more." It was the first work stoppage, and I led it, and a nonunion one.

My brother was the hog splitter. He was an artist, could split those ribs. And I was the header, a header of hogs. I was a fast butcher, very fast, and I wasn't the only one; there were others. When you work on a chain operation, everybody on that chain was a fast butcher. My brother said to me, "They're killing too many hogs today, let's walk—we're the two best butchers, two most important jobs." They were going at 350 an hour. I knew I could do 400, but you know, there are days when you just can't keep up. I said, "Charlie, we can't do that. Just think of what it would mean, to have two brothers who walked off this floor and caused damage to the company. Our names would spread everywhere, and probably we wouldn't get a job nowhere else. I'm going to quit; you stay here and work." I said to George Davis, my foreman, "Look, the chain is running too fast for me, give me some help, please. Today is not a good day for me." Davis said, "Phil, I am not going to give you any help, and I'm going to run these damn hogs by you so fast they're going to fan you!" When he said that, I hollered, "Hold the chain!" and somebody pressed a button, and the whole operation stopped. I just turned around at the bench, got my knives and steel, ran some water on them, and said, "You catch 'em, and let 'em fan you!"

In those days I guess I was somewhat of a damn fool. I didn't mind taking a punch at you, you know. You might knock me down and beat the hell of me, but you're going to get the fight of your life. You weren't going to get off light. And I was skinny; I was no big guy, nothing like that. But I didn't mind fighting if I believed in something. It was a part of my nature. As a kid I learned that there had to be strength in numbers. There was an innate feeling in me to be organized, to get people to believe in what I thought, and that together we could do something about these things.

Weightman's first experience with an official labor union was a negative one. He joined the Amalgamated Meat Cutters and Butcher Workmen during that union's post–World War I organizing campaign, but racial discrimination within the Amalgamated soon alienated Weightman. When the Meat Cutters struck the nation's packinghouses in the winter of 1921, very few African Americans rallied to its cause. After the strike was abandoned in January 1922, packinghouse unionism lay dormant till the mid-1930s.

You know they had a strike, the 1921 packing strike. It was a nasty thing. They lost. They lost, and we suffered humiliation. It was a paper union. They used to have booths, just like where they sell newspapers, where you come and pay your dues. No association with the workers, just a dues-collecting setup. No relationship.

I was there and paid my dues. I was a member of the Amalgamated. In that first Labor Day parade after the war, after the parade was over we were all lined up at our headquarters. I'm a youngster, lined up to get a sandwich. When I got up there, the guy looked at me and said, "We don't feed you in this line." I said, "What? You don't serve me in this line?" I looked over there, there were blacks in that line. I wasn't accustomed to that. In Mississippi, yeah, but I thought I had got away from that! I had participated with whites in doing things that ordinary blacks wouldn't do. I wasn't thinking about race—this, that, and the other race. What the hell! The question was fighting the boss, trying to get away from that twenty-seven and a half cents an hour! I didn't realize all of that—young and foolish, imbued with unionism and marching. So I walked out of that hall. That stayed in my craw; it was miserable. It destroyed my desire for unionism. I didn't want to see unionism coming or going. If somebody talked to me about a union, I would almost call him a bastard or something.

The debacle of the Amalgamated's defeat left deep scars. Like Weightman, most African American packinghouse workers continued to look askance at unionism, and whites blamed blacks for the defeat. Gertie Kamarczyk, who witnessed the strike as a 14-year-old canning room operative, recalled the depressed sense of resignation that followed the return to work:

We didn't understand why they went to work when we were out, and I guess they just couldn't trust the white people. We just didn't understand, and they didn't understand. We lost the union because of that, and I didn't think we was ever going to have one again, not with so many coloreds in there. I just thought I'd be slaving away till I died.[2]

35

For many black workers, though, the 1920s was a decade of genuine opportunity and economic advancement. Again, Phil Weightman's experience epitomized that of hundreds of other African Americans in the industry.

I went to work for the Krey Packing Company in 1926, after that incident where I walked off the job. I knew Mr. Krey, a small packer, because Krey Packing did not know how to perform the proper trims on hams and premium bellies. So they borrowed us guys who knew the trim from Swift, and I was one of those they borrowed. I trained their people how to do it. I went to Mr. Krey and said that I wanted a job. "Why, what's the matter? You quit Swift?" I said I sure did. "No, I'm not going to hire you. Phil, I could hire you today, and you'll go back to Swift tomorrow." "Well, Mr. Krey, all I can tell you is that I have quit Swift and I don't intend to go back." But the next two or three days he inquired as to whether I had gone back to Swift or not. He found out that I hadn't and he sent for me, and I went to work for him. And you know, he gave me seventy-one cents an hour, the top rate in his plant.

I worked for him through to 1929 when the Depression hit. You see, he had no guarantee. The big packers had first a forty-hour weekly guarantee, then they had a thirty-two hour week guarantee. But Krey had no guarantee. He gave his good butchers extra work in order to make up for a guarantee. But when the Depression hit, he didn't have the work to give us, and I went to him and told him that I was moving to Chicago. He shook his head and said, "Well, I'm going to say this to you. If you ever want to come back, just give me a call. You don't have the money, I'll send for you." I said, "I don't think you will have to do that." I knew that I excelled with a knife as a butcher, and there was no packing plant that wouldn't hire me.

When I came, I went to Armour's. A guy who lived in the house where I was, he worked for Armour. He said, come on out. I went out to Armour and Company. At that time, they killed something like a thousand hogs an hour on a conveyor. The man said, "What can you do?" "I can do anything." He looked at me. "The young punk can do anything! Can you head hogs?" "Yes." "Let me see you head a hog, that chain, three of them over there." I went over and did my thing, and it wasn't nothing like what they were doing. Mine was perfect; it didn't have any scratches or scars. He looked at that, looked at me, and said, "What did you say you could do?" I said, "Anything." "Can you split hogs?" "Yes I can." That gentleman waited till the big ones started coming by, and he sent me up there. He said, "Here, here's a cleaver. Let's see you split the hog." I split it right down the middle, didn't break a loin, didn't even scar it. That bone was split. He looked at me and said, "Come on . . ." There's a fancy job in the packinghouse known as facing hams. That's a very highly skilled job; you have to really know what you're doing. He said, "Let's see you do that." I did the fancy dandying! [laughs]

Soon as Armour had hired me, that man did everything in the world he could to keep me, but I was Swift orientated, you know. I went back over to

Swift for a job. They knew me by reputation, and they hired me. I liked Swift. When you work for Swift, you're more of a family. Swift and Company was owned by the Swift family. You see, I eventually came to know Harold Swift. The industrial relations department was seemingly a different kind of industrial relation department. No one could be swallowed. If you had ten years' service at Swift, you could not be fired except by the consent and approval of the general manager of the company. If you had problems, they had a fund set up for employee benefit. If an employee was having hard times, his rent was behind and he was about to be evicted, he could go to the company and ask for help, and they would pay at least one or two months of his rent. If he had a son or daughter that was in trouble with the law, Swift and Company would have one of its lawyers down at the court, to intercede if it was necessary. Swift and Company had a pension plan of its own. It wasn't that good. It was a pension plan mostly in name, but it was a pension plan. Now, in conjunction with that, Swift and Company was the hardest company to organize, because of the company's paternalism.

Despite his aversion to "the white man's union," within a few years Weightman was caught up in the CIO's campaign to organize Chicago's packinghouses. Although not a founder of PWOC Local 28, he soon emerged as its most visible black leader.

So while working at Swift, here came my reindoctrination into the unions. One day one of the guys in our plant, Hank Schoenstein, said to me, "Hey Phil, why don't you come with me. We're going to have a meeting—we want to start a union." I said, "I don't want to have anything to do with a goddamn union. I don't want to hear about it. Don't tell me nothing about a union." You know what was in my mind: back when the discrimination was shown.

When the organizing drive started in the Swift plant, I was a company man in every sense of the word. I was dealing with industrial relations elsewhere, building softball teams throughout the department and a baseball team that they were sponsoring from the Wabash YMCA. I went to them and said that I want a softball team for this department, will you give us some uniforms? Yes. And I set up a league, and so we had a Swift department softball league. I wanted a baseball team in the YMCA industrial league. They gave that to me, which I managed for many years, and bought uniforms and everything. Because I was a leader in sports, I was highly respected throughout the plant. The company respected me. I was an outspoken guy. I had that reputation, and for that reason Schoenstein thought I could help him organize the people and bring blacks into the Local 28.

OK, finally I decided to go to the meeting. I go to the meeting this night. I said, "Where is the meeting going to be?" "No, I can't tell you Phil. I'll take you." You know why they couldn't tell me—they had known me as a company man, and here I'm going to the meeting. How was they to know I wouldn't come back and tell the company where they were having the meeting? So I go to this meeting. And Lord God! What do you think they had? There were three men with Coca Cola cases to sit on. Three cases. One for me, one for this fellow that took me there, and the other. [laughing] That was the meeting! I said, "What the hell is this? Is this the meeting?"

So I went back in the plant a little discouraged and disgusted, but I told nobody about the meeting or anything. I went to several meetings, and the same thing was occurring. There was a guy working next to me named Carson. He was a fellow hog header, and this particular day the foreman came over to Carson and said, "Carson, I want to see you at the doctor's office." I said, "Have you been to the doctor, Carson? Something wrong with you?" "No." So he went to the doctor's office, and when he came back I said, "What happened?" He said, "Phil I'm fired." "What, you're fired? Why are you fired?" He said, "Swift and Company says I'm too great a risk. But they said they'll get me a job at another packinghouse." I went to my foreman and said, "Have you found any cause to feel that Carson is unable to do his job?" He said, "Wait a minute, Phil, I didn't have anything to do with this; this is the hand of the doctor. If the doctor say you can't work for Swift and Company, you can't work for Swift and Company." So I said, "That could apply to me. That could apply to anybody in here, right?" He said, "That's right."

So when I got to the next meeting, I said, "I don't want to be an organizer, but tonight I'm joining." I said, "How many members do you have?" "Oh, don't ask me that. I can't tell you that." "Well, the guys who are members, aren't they wearing their buttons?" "Well, we don't want them to wear their buttons, because they might get fired and we can't help them." I said, "OK, give me my button, give me about six buttons." The next morning the six buttons were put all around my cap! And my foreman walked up to that bench where I was working, and he saw that and he broke and run like a scared jackass! He went to the phone and called the division superintendent. And when he came up, he stood back a few minutes and gave me the intimidating look. Stood behind me and looked me up and he looked me down. And I'm laughing at him! I deliberately laughed at him! [laughs]

Then finally he came up and said to me, "Why did you join the union? Tell me one reason why did you join the union. You got everything you ask for." I said, "If I had asked you for a raise, could I have gotten that? I could ask you for a new towel, for some more soap in the washbasin, you would give me that. What about Carson? The doctor called Carson down and said he was a liability to Swift and Company, and you fired him. You can do that to any of us. If I can do anything about it, you ain't going to do that to me nor no one else. From this day on, everybody in this department, 120 workers, is going to be members of this union. I am going to see to that." From that time on, I was a belligerent, evil, cantankerous employee of Swift and Company, because they had mistreated a guy that I know was doing his job, because he was working beside me every day of his life. He and I both were doing the same job.

The most formidable challenge facing union activists at Swift and the other Chicago packinghouses in this period was overcoming the racial tensions and antagonisms stemming from the defeat of the 1921–1922 strike. John Wrublewski, a Polish American hog butcher who moved to Chicago in 1927, recalled his initial encounter with the racist attitudes and behavior of his workmates:

> When I first started the older white guys didn't talk to the Negroes, didn't share their locker room. Just wouldn't have anything to do with them. The guys on the floor who had gone through the strike was still nursing their wounds and their pride all them years later. It was eatin' away at them, and to hear them tell it, those Negroes had committed the greatest sin possible and there simply was no forgiveness, at least not in this world.[3]

In the Swift plant the rift between East European and black workers on the hog kill and elsewhere in the packinghouse was especially deep. Union activists succeeded in overcoming these divisions by organizing around workplace issues.

White workers were afraid to get into the union because they were scared of the blacks who might take their jobs in the event of a strike, because that had happened in a previous strike. The company had used blacks as strikebreakers in the packing industry—they brought these blacks in to break the union, and that was uppermost in the minds of the whites.

There was a couple of key Polish workers in my department. I went to them and I said, "I would like you to join the union, why don't you join?" He would look at me and say, "Phil, I'll join when that guy joins"—it was another black guy that he didn't trust. I could understand his feeling. I didn't cuss him out, no indeed. I courted him, tried to show him the benefits of union, the benefits of sticking together, and show him what I had done.

The sausage and sliced bacon departments were lily white, and the hardest to organize were the white women in the sausage room. I assigned Stanley Piontek, being Polish, to that area to organize, and he did it. Stanley had a way of convincing people, because he could talk about his own experiences. He was a beef boner, and at first Stanley refused to join the union. He shook his head, "No, there's too many black guys in it, too many black guys." I said, "What does that have to do with you, then? Join the union to help solve some of these problems. There are Polish people in the plant and Irish, so why don't you help me to get the Polish and Irish in, and you can be the majority?" I kept going by. I would go by his department but wouldn't go near him. Psyching him all the time. And it worked. One day somebody, I can't remember who, came and told me that Stanley had joined the union. I didn't go over and say anything to him. I just told the guy to tell him thanks, you know? I needed help.

The women in that sausage department bothered us more than anything else. Those women were combative; they seemed to want to scrap with each other, sometimes physically, and we had to deal with that. We had said we weren't going to tolerate that, and anybody that started fighting or bad-mouthing would be dealt with by the union. And if they were going to continually cause strife, we would recommend to management that they be discharged. You had such problems as these. I'll give you a mental picture: here's a chute, where trimmings come down to a table. Around this table there are women working, and they got hooks. These women are trimming the lean out of the fat, and they're grading it at the same time. They would get big bonuses—Swift and Company had the Bedaux system, the bonus system as they called it—and they would hit each others' hands, reach over the other with the hook for a big piece of meat that had a lot of lean in it, so she would get more poundage out of it. Another woman tried to start fighting to get it.

We had to break that up. We had the size of the table reduced, had the chute split off into different sections, and reduced the number being at one table. The same work but different sections. That is some of the problems. The other problems are that women have a tendency in certain times of the month to be ill, and the company just don't go out and hire somebody to replace that person, they go along until they get all right, because it's only a couple of days or so. But the other women's got to carry that load, you see: "Sister Mary's sick today. We're going to keep her here on the job, but we're going to carry her."

We had to develop that. We created an impression that the boss is your enemy and the fellow worker beside you is not your enemy. It's only him, it's that boss, he's your enemy. He's the guy that gives you orders, he's the guy that writes your time out, he's the fellow who recommends your discharge. About the only thing he don't do is hire you, but he can get rid of you. So we must all get it in our eyes that when one's in trouble, all's in trouble. Stanley did a whole lot of that, and Stanley brought that department almost a hundred percent. We did organize those white women. Most people don't want to fight for themselves, but they're glad if somebody will fight for them. Sometimes you will find they will join you, but somebody got to start it for them. I'm telling you, Stanley was great.

The forging of solidarity was a gradual process. Ethnic chauvinism resurfaced from time to time, especially in the formative years of the PWOC. In 1939, Chicago's packinghouse workers formed a citywide body to better coordinate their efforts to unionize the plants in the stockyards. Nationalist sentiment threatened the viability of this project.

We had a Packinghouse Workers Joint Council here in Chicago. We had one hell of a fight to keep them from setting up a Polish committee and a black committee; different divisions in there. One night I had to filibuster about two hours. My argument was, we're going to have one union or we're not going to have a union at all. I knew if they got a Polish division there was going to be blacks and Polish fighting like mad for positions, and as long as I could keep any and all divisions out, I thought we might have a union.

You had black workers that you were trying to organize at that same time that you were organizing the whites. We could not cater to the whites and we could not cater to the blacks. What we had to do was to say, this is the principle on which this union is organized: no second-class citizenship; everybody who pays his dues are members of this union and will be protected to the degree that is possible to protect you. We never met with a black group or a white group; it was always bringing together.

We built a fraternity in Swift and in the packinghouses in general. It got to the point when a Polish member would die, or some member of a family of a Polish member would die, you know who they wanted to go and say the last words? Me. If they were sick I would go see them. I would have greetings sent from the local union or from me. We had a good relationship.

The UPWA's second convention, held in Omaha in 1944, sent a strong message to the membership about the commitment to equality and interracial unity. When the hotel hosting the convention refused to house black delegates, packinghouse leaders moved the meeting into the cramped union hall despite stifling 102-degree heat. Those present for the four-day conclave never forgot this inspired protest. For many whites, this was their first encounter with racial discrimination. "I think they would have preferred being in the Hotel Continental where we were supposed to be," one participant remembered, "but they did it, and there's a learning process in there." Weightman vividly recalled this episode.[4]

We made arrangements at the hotel for the convention without looking into its racial practices or anything. We ought to have known in that time and period that there was a racial problem in Omaha, but somehow or another we were so imbued in what we were doing with the Packinghouse Workers union we didn't think of that. So we went out there. First thing they wanted was that I couldn't stay in the hotel. Next they wanted the delegation and myself to come up in the back elevator! So we decided there ain't going to be no convention here, not at this hotel!

So the membership in Omaha was in the process of buying a building for their headquarters there, a local center. They said, "We'll show 'em, we'll have it in our own building!" We ended up having the convention in that local union hall. And we all stayed in packinghouse workers' homes. It was grand. It wasn't a luxurious affair or anything like that. You can understand, though, standing up in that sort of situation made your union strong from a racial standpoint, and that's what happened there.

Many things happened to us to make us strong; we didn't succumb to it. We had a conference in Des Moines, Iowa, on one occasion. We sat down in a restaurant to eat. I'm sitting there so I ordered. Everybody else ordered. Somebody says, "Phil, did you order?" I said yes. "Did they bring you any tools [silverware]?" No. So, we fixed it. They waited till they brought the meals and all were served, everybody around the table, and then they said, "Where's his?" "We can't serve him." We all got up as a team and walked out. See, that helps to make a union too. I mean there was only one black. They could have said, "Well Phil, I'm sorry, we've got our breakfast, you go and eat at a table somewhere." Nothing like that.

Herbert March

While Philip Weightman and other activists were building an inclusive industrial union at Swift, unionists across the yards at the giant Armour plant were struggling to weld together their workmates into an interracial alliance. Much of the progress made at Armour was due to the dynamism of a young white activist, Herbert March.

Born in Brooklyn in 1913, March became involved in labor organizing through his membership in the Young Communist League. In 1933 he moved to Chicago and began working at Armour and Company where he set about building the Packinghouse Workers Industrial Union, one of the many precursors to the PWOC. Perhaps more than any other single individual, March was responsible for the creation of strong bonds of solidarity between white and black workers in Chicago. He believed that packinghouse workers' shared experience on the job provided the common ground upon which interracial unionism could be built and that union action against racial discrimination was necessary to demonstrate the PWOC's commitment to equality.

Since World War I, a significant number of black workers had been in the industry. They had worked side by side with white workers on the killing and cutting floors. Instead of having workers who were just off a farm, you had an industrialized group of black workers who had all this experience of exploitation. And there was all sorts of discrimination practice against them. From the inception our union kept fighting against the discrimination and was able to win the confidence of the black workers.

This whole concept of black-white unity was at the heart of the organization. For instance, the union adopted the black and white hand clasp as the emblem of the organization, and we had black and white staff as soon as we were able to get staff in the organization. And the idea of black and white unity became a central factor. For instance, one of the first grievances we

Herbert March speaking at a January 1952 rally in the Chicago stockyards. *Photo courtesy of Herbert March.*

took up at Armour was a demand that the company remove from the time card of the workers who were black a little asterisk, a star. The star became an anathema as far as they were concerned, because what would happen with frequent turnover and layoffs in the meatpacking industry, a foreman would get instructions to lay off so many men. The foremen were all white, and they would look over the time cards, and they would pick out the cards where there was a star. Those were the fellows who got laid off. So one of the first demands was that they remove stars from the cards—that everybody be treated equally—and we won that demand. They removed the star from the time cards of the black workers. Things like that helped create both unity and confidence and mutual trust of the white and black workers.

Partly due to his left-wing connections, March was able to draw upon an alternative historical memory of the 1921–1922 strike, one that stressed the union movement's accomplishments in bringing blacks and whites together in the tense period between the 1919 Chicago Race Riot and the ill-fated strike. By providing workers with a sense of their own history, union activists emphasized the need for solidarity.

The union did a good job of countering an attempt to split the workers on the basis of their color with the 1921 situation. The guys always talked about how during the race riot Jack Johnstone, who was then active as organizer and chief griever in the Stockyards Labor Council, organized this checkerboard parade of white and black through the southside and developed the idea of black and white unity. And one of the first things the guys very consciously did when we started to build the union was bringing in the black guys, giving them leadership posts. From the beginning. It just made sense that if you're going to have a union, everybody's got to be in it and we've got to work together.

And they saw that the black guys were very, very active, and a lot of them were articulate. Especially at the beginning there were a lot of young blacks in the packinghouses who had college degrees. They went to work in the packinghouses because it's all you could do. You were lucky if you got that. And so a lot of them played that role.

So from the inception, we initiated the union and developed the union and carried it through as a union of black and white workers. It was part of your life; it was accepted. It wasn't a question of whites trying to bring forward blacks; it was just an integral part of the union and its thinking from the word go. Some of our first problems and issues that arose were because of our insistence on that. For example, I remember one of the first things that happened when we started to organize. Walter Strabawa from the pork pack of Armour's, which was half Polish workers and about half black, got married at St. Rose of Agnes Church. It was in the heart of the Polish community. And a bunch of workers from his department, from the pork section, came to be there at the wedding, and a large number of them were black, and there some ushers at the church made them unwelcome. And we ended up with a protest at the church.

Indivisible from his activities as a union organizer were Herb March's efforts to build a Communist presence in the stockyards. Working with his wife, Jane, and a handful of other activists, March built a strong Party unit that supported the union campaign in a variety of ways. Of great importance were the recruits it drew from a younger cohort of black workers that entered the industry when employment picked up after 1935. Many of these workers had previous contact with the Left through experience in the movement to organize the unemployed in the early 1930s and in the mass campaigns that developed around the defense of Angelo Herndon and the Scottsboro Boys. In this radical milieu, they learned to work closely with white allies, acquired specific organizational skills, and gained a respect for the leadership of the Communist Party with regard to black issues.

One such recruit, Lowell Washington, first encountered Communists when as a teenager he became involved in an effort to organize Works Progress Administration workers. "Those guys really threw me," he remembered. "I mean here were these white fellas who were helping us out, really meaning it. I'd never seen anything like it." The critical factor in his attraction to the leftists was their grievance approach to organizing. "They took up the things that really mattered—jobs, food, places to live," he explained. "You might not agree with them all the time, but you had to stand with 'em when they was fightin' for you. You'd be a fool not to."[5]

Like Washington, many future black packinghouse unionists took part in Communist-led demonstrations in the early 1930s. For many these were critical formative experiences. Todd Tate, a burly six-foot-six giant of a man who later served as a steward in the Armour plant, joined many "flying squadrons" that mobilized to prevent rent evictions. It was in this capacity that he first met Richard Saunders, a union founder at the Armour Soap Works, and Leon Beverly, later president of that local. Saunders recalled that Communist speakers provided him with the "method and know-how" that allowed him to organize on the job. "Some of the things they would preach I could pick up on and go back in my plant and institute." Although never a Party member, Saunders felt an affinity with the Communists. "The thing was issues, the issues that were important to people. And these guys dealt with issues." This outspokenness, especially with regard to black equality, led Saunders to join the Communist-sponsored John Brown Society, an organization primarily composed of young people who "preached the doctrine that the only way for working people—black, white, and what have you—was to organize and break down these racial barriers and differences and unite our forces."[6]

By the close of the Depression decade, the Communists exercised considerable influence over Chicago Armour Local 347 and had begun to "colonize" in the Swift and Wilson plants. They made major contributions to the advance of the organization campaigns in these packinghouses, but their presence provoked controversy. Phil Weightman carefully explained the reasons behind his distrust of the Communists but, significantly, went out of his way to praise their contributions to the union cause and the struggle for black equality.

Philip Weightman

We knew that in order to organize packing, [CIO President] John L. Lewis had recruited as many Communist organizers as he could find and put them in key positions. Lewis didn't give a damn whether the Communists controlled it or not; he was just interested in organizing the industry. Now I was opposed to Communism as such, because of their nature to take over such things as the secretary-treasurer's job and to control the union. Now, the leadership that developed in our union decided that, so what, let them help us organize! We'll work with them all, but we're going to make certain that they don't take over this union.

The Communists felt that they had better recruit me. The black worker was this country's Achilles' heel so far as the Party was concerned, and they looked upon me as their fair-haired boy that they could use, and really ran after me good. My God! There was a restaurant right off Ashland Avenue where we would have lunch or have dinner, sit down and talk after a meeting at the union headquarters. They offered to write my speeches if they knew I was going to go somewhere to speak. Write my speeches for me! And hand it me, or put it in an envelope and give it to me. Or if they didn't write the total speech, then they would include in the speech certain things they thought that I should talk about during the course of my speech. Boy!

I never became a member of the Party—each time I refused. There was a guy on the staff named John Hackney. Hackney came to my office one day and said, "Tell me, why, why you don't join the Party?" I said, "I don't want to join the Party because I don't think it's good for me, I don't think it's good for black people; I just don't think it's good."

Now, in saying all of that, the Communist Party pushed programs. They talked interracial. Anti-discrimination. They did something after I was out that I had been trying to do while I was there: to catch Swift in the act of discrimination. The Local 28 Communist leadership tricked Swift and Company. They sent in some people to be hired in the employment office. Swift said there were no jobs available. They sent some whites in right behind them, and the same jobs were available and they were hired. And as a result of the suit, they got a case where Swift and Company paid a couple of hundred people or more. It was the Communist Party who did that. I give them credit for that. I have no animosity against any of it. These are the kind of things that I can say the Communist Party helped.

In all I've said about the Communists, I don't want to take anything away from them. They contributed. I may not have been as aggressive as I was if it hadn't been for them, you see? The fact that they were talking and urging this, that, and the other, that I thought was for the wrong reasons, but they were good things that they were suggesting. That makes the difference.

Sam Parks and Charles Hayes

Sam Parks and Charles Hayes were part of the second phase of the Great Migration that took place in the 1940s. Both men joined a large cohort of African Americans who entered the Chicago packinghouses during World War II. More militant than the generation of black workers that preceded them, and more optimistic about the promise of a dynamic interracial labor movement, this wartime group proved especially receptive to the overtures of the Communist Left.

Born in Memphis, Tennessee, Sam Parks moved to Chicago in 1940. While studying law at night, he worked first in a coke plant and then as a construction laborer before entering the Wilson plant in 1941. Charles Hayes migrated to Chicago from Cairo, Illinois, where he had built levees on the Mississippi River with the Civilian Conservation Corps, labored as a railroad section hand, and stacked wood in a lumber yard. Entering the Wilson plant at about the same time, Parks and Hayes began to organize their workmates around an aggressive program of action-oriented shop-floor unionism. They soon attracted a significant following among workers impatient with the weak leadership provided by Local 25's existing officers.

In 1944, a slate headed by Parks and Hayes captured control of Local 25 and moved to solidify the union's position in the plant. With Parks as president and Hayes serving as chair of the grievance committee, the local used direct-action tactics to bring Wilson to the bargaining table, eliminate segregation, and combat discriminatory hiring practices. Along with white leftists in the mechanical gangs, they also moved the Wilson local firmly into an alliance with the Left-led Armour local.

Sam Parks

During World War II, I went to Wilson and got a job as a freezer man; that's the department that freezes the meat after the slaughtering process. At that time they had a local CIO union with a black guy by the name of Dock Williams as president and a white woman, Mary Wilson, as a secretary-treasurer. And they were a company union, although they had a CIO label and everything else. Dock was a limited black man, with very little academic training, very little, but a lot of black bullshit charisma in the style of a black preacher etcetera, and therefore Dock kept the blacks in line in the local. Mary Wilson, she kept the whites in line. Both of them were anti–Herb March and the Left.

I started working in the freezer and noticed certain working conditions that weren't right. I spoke up about 'em, and continued to speak up about

Sam Parks, about 1958. *Used with permission of the State Historical Society of Wisconsin* *[WHi (X3) 50375].*

'em. My mind was not on any involvement in the union; my mind was on getting a sheep skin—I had enrolled at John Marshall Law School and was taking up law. I was going to get to be a lawyer quick, and after I got my degree in law I was going to fuck over, freak up, rob Negroes, make me some money and get rich. That was in my mind. I wanted to get rich quick through the black avenue. But by being there, working every day in that environment, you take up grievances, you got to be affected by them. The guys started to clamor for me to be the steward in that department. So, finally I relented and I became the steward.

They treated workers in that Wilson plant just like I happened to see when I was a kid living in the South in Memphis, the way I saw white people treat workers down there. And I figured, hell, this is Chicago! This is supposed to be the home of freedom. Ain't no white man got no business doing no Negro that way up here. So I started to protest at the manner and the way that the white foremen related to the black workers. I called for a sit-down in our department until we got grievances settled. Management threatened to fire me, but when they threatened to fire me all of the guys walked out and said they wouldn't touch anything, and they wouldn't allow Dock Williams or Mary Wilson to negotiate for me. Once I started protesting, it started spreading. Other cases come up in other departments of the plant.

I started to fighting Dock with my department, and I fought and I fought, and I saw to it to go into the local union meetings, challenging him on different things and everything else. So then the election rolled around in 1944, and people started asking me about running for president of the local. I ran and I won based upon the fact that I thought that there ought to be new leadership. Now my intention at that time was not to continue to be a trade union leader. I was running in order to step down; somebody else can step up and I continue to pursue my degree in law. But life has it that sometimes as an individual you do not always determine your own fate. And getting engrossed and enthused, and having a certain amount of egotism myself, well hell, it got to me, OK? I'm admitting it.

Charles Hayes

Charles Hayes began working at the Wilson plant just a few months before Sam Parks. Like Parks, he was a relative newcomer to Chicago, having moved there during the early war years in search of employment opportunity, and had no intention of pursuing a career in the labor movement. Events overtook him, however. In 1944 he joined forces with Parks to oust the older, conservative leadership of Local 25. At that time, he considered the Wilson UPWA local no better than a "company union." Prior to moving to Chicago, Hayes labored at a lumber company in Cairo where he helped found an interracial union local, an experience that helped prepare him for the task ahead in meatpacking.

Back in 1939 I managed to get this job at E. L. Bruce, a hardwood flooring company. I first started off as a yard worker—all they did was stack the lumber. The lumber would come in green, and they would stack it in the yard so it would dry with the sun. My job was to jack the lumber up to a guy who was stacking it. I didn't stay there but a few months. They needed someone to work inside the mill, tying the flooring together, and I started there, with no union, nothing.

I had read something about unions, heard something about them, and I knew it was suicide to try to take your grievances up on a one-on-one basis with the employer. It was a matter of human dignity. I was young; I wanted a job, but I wanted to be treated like a human being, and I didn't feel the guys were being treated that way. Just wanted to protect ourselves. Since we were working with lumber, we decided the best thing to do was to join the carpenters' union. I understood enough to write a letter—took $2.50 of my salary that I was making, got four other guys to join me, sent it to the carpenters' union in Indianapolis, and applied for a charter.

We had signed up all the black workers. But they wouldn't recognize us. The only way we got recognition was a strike, and since the company was based in Memphis, Tennessee, the superintendent who ran our plant had no authority anyway to recognize us or sign a contract with us. So after striking we finally got called to Memphis to sit down and negotiate our first contract. And after we had gone through the business of a strike, the white workers decided that they would join in with us. Because they had certain grievances too; the wages were low for them, although not as low as ours. And actually they were dependent upon us; although they had better jobs, machine operators and things of this sort, they couldn't operate the machines if no lumber was available for them, so they recognized that, and they joined in with us. That's the way I got started. I remained the president of Local 1424 of the Carpenters' Union around two years

I had an uncle from Chicago who came down every year to visit. He had been telling me that he could get me a job where he was working in Wilson's smoked meat department. And I took the chance. Came to Chicago in 1942, got me a room, and got me a job. I started working in the fresh pork department, placing meat on the table for pork boners and then hauling the meat away when they got a truck full of it. It was a laborer's job. The wages were better than we were making in Cairo. I left Cairo at about 25 cents an hour, but when I got to the stockyards I made 67 and a half cents an hour, which was a big deal at that time.

They were in the process of trying to organize a union. In the main stockyards, Armour was already organized; Swift I believe was already organized at that time; and several of these so-called independent meatpackers were organized. Wilson was a more difficult one because they had what they called an independent union; it was nothing but a company union, that's what it was. The leadership was dominated by the company. The grievance procedure was almost nonexistent And they would fire you with little or no recourse. We in Wilson's did not have the kind of solidarity and unity that was prevalent in Armour because of the existence of the company union. That was one thing that you had to always be conscious of.

Dock Williams was the president of the company union. His power to some extent was illusionary. The company would certainly listen to him, because he was offering no real resistance to them, and he could meet almost whenever with the company. But in terms of being able to solve the real grievances of people, if you're a part of that inner clique, I guess you could get something done, but when you got beyond that, well there wasn't very much to hope for in the way of change.

We were trying to get rid of this union because it was controlled primarily by the company. But in order to do it, you had to get people signed up who wanted to be represented by the Packinghouse Workers Organizing Committee. I joined in with those who were working in this direction. Having this experience I had in Cairo, it was just easy for me to be a part of this move, even though when I went there I had no intention of staying in the stockyards. Heck, the farthest thought in my mind was to take up the cudgels of a union again. All I could think of was becoming some kind of a skilled worker. I had left Cairo and came here with the thought of working a while and then going to school, but the color of my skin and the fact that I had no money were barriers that stood in the way.

The racial division of labor within the plant helps explain which departments supported the rank-and-file movement within the Wilson local and which ones held back. As in so many other packinghouses, the killing floors, with their concentrations of black and Hispanic workers, proved critical.

The core of support for the union came from the killing floors, coupled with the loading docks and the freezer department—that's where I first met Sam Parks. Those people worked under extreme conditions. They were most anxious to try to get out from under that bondage that they were working under.

On the other hand, there were certain areas in the plant, certain departments, where you were just blocked out. You take the nicer departments where the cleaner and better jobs existed, like the bacon department, they were mostly white. They were not anxious for the union. People who worked in the mechanical department felt that they were doing very well. The company was able to keep us separated just based on the fact that they had the better jobs, and they kept them feeling that if you get the union in there's going to be a threat to you. You're going to have work around with some of these black folks and this kind of stuff. Some of them sort of fell for that, but they eventually changed.

Under Parks and Hayes's leadership, the Wilson local began to combat the discriminatory assignation of jobs, working to open previously all-white departments to blacks. The most effective weapon was the use of direct-action tactics by the work gangs on the critical killing floors.

51

Sam Parks

The sliced bacon department was all lily-white women; the mechanical department was all lily-white men. Dock Williams didn't care. Dock never sent no Negroes to sliced bacon. No Negroes worked in them clean, good departments. Where Negroes worked was the hog offal—that's where the guts and bowels all spill down. Hog kill, beef kill, beef offal, fertilizer department—those were the black jobs in that plant. And I started a crusade. I sent the hog kill down to the company to grieve, to force them to hire some black women in sliced bacon.

I led a bunch of black workers, beef kill and hog kill, with blood on 'em and every other mother-fuckin' thing and went into the Wilson office and we sat all on top of the fuckin' desks. Scared the shit out of the superintendent and everybody else. All of them black workers with knives, blood dripping, sweat, scared them poor white women in that office to death! They were screaming; they figured a revolution had come! I said we're not moving till you give us an agreement. And we sat there while they called the national office of Wilson. The answer was, they would hire black women. They had to do it, because I had 'em by their balls. No packing plant's worth a damn without the ability to process the meat. The sliced bacon? You can't slice no bacon if we don't kill no hogs! So I had 'em. And after we got blacks in there, then the white workers saw the strength; they saw that naked power. This was supermilitant action now.

Stoppages of this nature were controversial. With American entry into World War II, the CIO guaranteed not to strike in return for a modified closed shop and the employers' automatic checkoff of workers' union dues. Throughout the meat-packing industry, though, job actions continued throughout the war years. In contrast to many other CIO unions, this reflected the transmission of a militant shop-floor tradition to newcomers rather than a weakening of the union's influence over its members. Herbert March commented that as a result, "we had an experience of building our union up through the period of the war which involved this constant stoppage, slow-down, fighting around issues. Constant militancy around issues was at the heart of the functioning of the union, and this had as a result a rank and file that was unusually militant."

Like many packinghouse activists, Sam Parks drew a distinction between job actions and the sort of walkouts that would have violated the no-strike agreement. Significantly, he linked the issues of patriotism and racial prejudice.

I didn't close the plant. Close the plant then I'm in violation of the no-strike pledge and I'm unpatriotic. Close the plant then I'm interested in Hitler winning the war. And God knows Hitler would copy his shit from [U.S. Senator Theodore] Bilbo in Mississippi—that's where German Aryan supremacy comes from, down in Mississippi. I'll not support Hitler. I'll be accused of supporting Hitler if I closed the whole plant. Our country is at war and they need the meat. But to strike this department and the rest of the plant worked, you can't say I'm unpatriotic. That was the technique.

A similar dynamic prevailed in the Swift plant. Leaders like Weightman, a degree more cautious than men like Parks, responded to the no-strike pledge in a similar if less dramatic fashion.

Philip Weightman

We kept our no-strike pledge at the Swift plant, but you have to stand your ground. Because of their long experience, workers in the cattle killing department dressed 150 an hour—that's about the highest speed the cattle would go. That's 1,200 in eight hours. The workers became so proficient that instead of doing that in their regular hours, they did that in six and a half or seven hours. They did the eight hours' work and took off. Management endorsed that for a long time. Then all of a sudden they had them doing that and paying them for seven hours' work. So the workers got mad. I said, "OK, let's do some planning. If they want to take an hour and a half pay away from you, go on and slow down. Remember we got a no-strike pledge. Slow it down; take nine hours to do it, but keep working. So remember that guy with a stopwatch, the Bedaux man that comes around, timing you? If you keep operating, if you keep moving, there's no loss of motion. All they're doing is a motion study. Keep your hands going on something, but don't let them be doing nothing." Damn thing! We slowed it down, and they restored that time to them. That's some of the job actions that we had. You had to do it. Kept them in the plant. There was nobody going out on strike; they just slowed down.

One of the more significant developments in the stockyards in the 1940s was the expansion of Communist influence. The alliance between African American packinghouse workers and the Communists was a complex one, forged as much out of pragmatism as ideological affinity.

Sam Parks

After I won the presidency, I started cooperating with the white Left leaders of the district—Herb March and other white leaders. I cooperated with Herb and other white leaders, not because of Herb being a national member of the Communist Party, not because some of the other whites around him were so politically inclined. I cooperated with them because I saw at that time that they were interested in fighting for blacks to get better jobs inside the plant, and I knew that would benefit most of the black workers. I was interested in the black masses, and I thought these guys had the right answer for the advancement of the black masses. I worked with them over the years, and they did make a hell of a contribution in the direction of tearing down discrimination in the packing industry. And it couldn't have been done by the black workers alone in the union; it had to be done by the black and whites working together in the packing union. I embraced the ideology of Left progressive thinking people, black and white, because I thought it was in the best interests of black people in particular, and black and white people generally. Remember how I put this: black people in particular, and black and white people generally. I put our cause first.

The thing that made the Packinghouse Workers a progressive union was the combination of blacks and the white Left. The Communists and the blacks, that's what made it. And there were the whites in the union that weren't Communist, but they still were progressive. I think that the Left whites and the Communist whites helped to make a hell of a difference in that union: standing out as an example, cooperating and working with blacks, and then talking to a lot of white workers in the plant. If it hadn't have been for that, the Packinghouse Workers union wouldn't have been any different from any other union. One has to pay tribute to where tribute is due. I think Herb March made a hell of a contribution to the advancement of blacks in this union. He made a hell of a contribution. If it hadn't have been for guys like Herb working with guys much like myself and other blacks, then the Packinghouse union wouldn't have had the progressive policies and programs that it had.

Entering into an alliance with the Left opened up unionists to right-wing attacks. Charles Hayes explained that despite such assaults, black workers proved resistant to the appeals of anti-communism.

Charles Hayes

They were calling us Communists and everything else at that time, left-wingers, and stooges of Herb March and the Communist Party. But our way prevailed because we kept saying that we had to have a union that the people controlled. No one liked to be besmudged, but it didn't hurt that much to be accused of being a left-winger. Black folks didn't get caught up in the syndrome of looking under the rug in every room for a red. It just didn't ring a bell with them. We wanted to get free. I don't care who helps us, help us, you know, that was the general attitude.

But I don't think you should give the C.P. credit for getting the union off the ground. I think it was the determination and the perseverance of the people themselves. The white people who were part of the union had it pounded into them: if we were going to get some of what we deserved and wanted, it was only through unity we were going to do it. That kind of preaching. So I don't say that the pride of authorship for that kind of togetherness necessarily emanated from the Communist Party.

The Packinghouse Workers bitter 1948 strike strained the interracial and interethnic solidarity that the union had built since the mid-1930s. It also tested the UPWA's relationship with various community organizations as well as the leadership of the Communists in the Chicago district.

Although violence flared at regular intervals during the 13-week conflict, it did not assume a racialized character; instead, it tended to be aimed at the packers, the police, or individual strikebreakers. Support from the black community and the Back-of-the-Yards neighborhood was impressive and helped the union weather the storm of injunctions and police-sanctioned picket line violence. Assistance lent by the Catholic Church proved especially important.

Philip Weightman

We had a good relationship with the Back-of-the-Yards Council and Bishop Sheil. The Catholic Church helped us with the strike—the Catholic priests rescued our picket line from the raiding of the police force, which was a beautiful thing to behold. We knew Captain Barnes [head of the Chicago Red Squad] was lining up a whole corps of police to raid our picket line. We got in touch with Saul Alinsky and said this is what's happening, please get in touch with Bishop Sheil and tell him to have some priests out there—if nothing else, witnesses to what's going to happen to us, because they intended to really do us in. The next morning, here come all of these big Cadillacs driving over with all these guys! And they were the priests! [laughing] The priests were the ones who were carrying the picket signs! Most beautiful thing that you could ever see. The priests were carrying the picket signs! You're talking about some disgusted policemen!

Impressive as such unity may have been, it was not enough. Crippled by the recently passed Taft-Hartley Act, the refusal of the Truman administration to intervene in the dispute, and the determined efforts of the packers to crush the UPWA, the strike crumbled. The defeat, although resounding, did not spell the demise of the union.

Charles Hayes

The company just outlasted us, there's no question about it. It was a vicious thing. They broke the strike and fired us leaders because they saw it as an opportunity to bust the union. Fire us leaders, you know, you cut off a snake's head, the tail will soon die—that was the theory behind it. But those people did not give out on the union after they went back. For a while we had disunity among ourselves. Some of the people felt that it was ill advised to have stayed out as long as we did and were mad at the union, but the majority of them felt that whatever mistakes might have been made, we still need the organization. We had to go through another representation election, and we won it again because people realized that they couldn't work for Wilson without a union. Wilson was a rough outfit, a rough outfit.

The 1948 strike marked a turning point in the careers of Philip Weightman, Sam Parks, and Charles Hayes. Publicly identified with the right-wing "CIO Policy Caucus" within the UPWA, Weightman was defeated for reelection as International vice president after the fierce internal factional battle that followed the strike. He left the union and went to work for the national CIO, overseeing political action campaigns around the country.

Fired by Wilson, Sam Parks first served as a business agent for the Wilson local before moving on to head the UPWA Chicago District's Anti-Discrimination Committee. His supermilitancy, independence, and penchant for confrontational activism often placed him in conflict with both the white Left and the more moderate elements in the union bureaucracy.

Sam Parks

When the strike came, I was fired, along with some other black stewards and stewardesses. I was through, and I knew that, so far as Wilson was concerned. I got fired because of the grip I had on the local. I had Herb March, Jesse Prosten, and [UPWA President Ralph] Helstein tell me that I shouldn't be full-time for my local; I ought to go back in the plant and put my overalls on. But it wasn't them that carried the strength in the plant, it was me.

I didn't put my overalls on. I stayed out and became a local business agent; and I wore my good suits. Good clothes. And I wore 'em because down in Memphis I never did get 'em. Goin' to live good. They told me I ought to go back, and a meeting was called of my local. And you would have thought that the people in that room was getting ready to lynch anybody that said any damn thing about me going anywhere. They were defying the Left white leadership that wanted to dominate black people in that union.

I happened to be their pride and joy, their baby boy, let me put it that way, and you couldn't get rid of me in that fashion.

If I hadn't been supermilitant, I'd have been on the staff. If I'd have kissed some white ass, I'd have been on the staff. If I'd have grinned, bowed, I'd have been on the staff. I didn't. If you subdued your militancy and conformed, then you stayed. But if you didn't, you had to go. Charlie [Hayes] was put on the staff, and he became the spokesman for blacks in the district.

Wilson discharged Charles Hayes during the 1948 strike as well. He subsequently joined the staff of Chicago District 1. In 1954, Hayes successfully ran for the post of district director.

Charles Hayes

Well, I didn't actually push for it really. I had served as a field representative for the union from '49 for five years, and there was an increasing feeling developing that the majority of the members in the district was black, why not have a black person to head up the district organization? That feeling was prevalent throughout. We had reached a point where we thought that the mantle of leadership could go to a black in this district. We looked at the whole board of our international union, and we had a guy out in California named Sonny Morrison who was black, and that same year we had a guy named George Thomas who was going after Pittman [Director of the Southwestern District], which we all loved! And what about Chicago, with this preponderance of black members here, why shouldn't we?

It made sense. And I guess I was selected because I was categorized as having a level head, one who had a pretty good power, and one who would be acceptable to the most folk, white and black.

In the early 1950s, black activists in the Chicago UPWA pushed the anti-discrimination program beyond the plants into the larger community. Some of their first targets were the restaurants and taverns in the stockyards district frequented by packinghouse workers.

The area surrounding the stockyards wasn't too conducive to too much race mixing. The taverns were segregated; restaurants were segregated, except for one instance right across from the Wilson plant. Right across the street there used to be restaurants we couldn't go into as blacks. [Saul] Alinsky and some of the others in the Back-of-the-Yards Neighborhood Council joined with us and helped to break down some of those conditions. I can remember at 46th and Ashland how we went in that eatery and demanded service. Told them we weren't going to move until we were served. They called the police, and they were scared to put us in jail. For what? It was a public place. They finally relented, they served us. That's the way we got it broke down. Of course we got some help from the NAACP and others.

Packinghouse workers and their allies from other area industrial unions transformed the Chicago branch of the NAACP in this period, enrolling hundreds of unionists and electing autoworker Willoughby Abner president. Previously, the Association had not been particularly responsive to working-class concerns. "They were very straightlaced," observed Todd Tate, who recalled that workers regarded the NAACP as a "silk-stocking," "tea sipping" organization that operated in a world far removed from their own.

The effort to turn the NAACP into an active ally of the city's black working class originated in 1948 as part of the Progressive Party movement within the ranks of organized labor.

Sam Parks

I ran on the Progressive Party ticket against Congressman [William] Dawson. I was the only candidate on the Progressive Party ticket in the whole State of Illinois when Henry Wallace ran. During the days of the Progressive Party in '48, it became apparent that the local NAACP was being dominated by the political forces of Congressman Dawson. The NAACP chapter in Chicago was run by Dawson. So, being a member of the Progressive Party, and being a candidate for office and everything else, well, I suggested to the leaders of our union, and other unions too, that we should infiltrate the NAACP and vote in a progressive leadership. And thus we got our stewards and our members to become members. Therefore a struggle took place inside the NAACP among the Right and the Left; we were the Left. And in some of the NAACP meetings we outvoted other forces.

Although increasingly involved in community-wide mobilizations, packinghouse activists concentrated their efforts on the struggle to improve conditions in the areas frequented by UPWA members on a day-to-day basis.

Charles Hayes

There was Goldblatt's—a lot of packinghouse workers had accounts at Goldblatt's and some of the other stores in the area, and they had to know that we were reaching a point where you aren't going to be able to continue to take our money if you're going to treat us this way. Sam and myself and a woman named Flo—she used to be a secretary in the Wilson local—we just went in there, sat down at that little lunch counter, and the waitress didn't want to serve us. The manager came down, and Sam raised so much hell in that store I think the walls were vibrating!

As told by Sam Parks, the Goldblatt's incident revealed divisions within the union and among its allies, many of whom preferred equally as determined but less confrontational tactics. The aggressive technique used at Goldblatt's was applied subsequently to other targets.

Sam Parks

The Goldblatt's store at 47th and Ashland—used to go in there, the white waitresses take their time waiting on you, sometimes they ignore you. I pulled a sit-down at the counter. Another two people were with me. We came to the counter, and the lady kept on waiting, waiting on the white people at this end, and there ain't no waitress at that end. She ain't waiting on us! And when she ain't no waiting on us, I hollered goddamn it, she goin' to wait on ourselves or she ain't going to wait on no goddamn body else in here. And I jumped up, I started walking, dared anybody to come and take a seat. You a white person, no, you ain't sitting here to eat! The policy of this store is that they're going to feed everybody, and they ain't going to discriminate.

The store got hold of Joe Meegan, who was head of the Back-of-the-Yard Council, and he came over. "Get up." I ain't gettin' no goddamn up I told him, fuck you! He went and got a hold of Helstein. Helstein sent word: "Get up or you're through." I sent word back there, "Kiss my ass, I ain't moving." And we kept on there until the head of the Goldblatt chain came out, one of the old Goldblatt brothers, and promised me, "Mr. Parks, from now on you all will be able to sit in any Goldblatt store in the city of Chicago and eat like dignified ladies and gentlemen." I shook his hand and said thank you and that was the end of it.

A little bit later than this Goldblatt thing, I was head of the Anti-Discrimination department for the packing union; I was also regional vice president of the National Negro Labor Council. We started a program and we targeted major industries: the airlines, the department stores, the banks, and the major corporate executive offices for blacks to work in, because back in 1950 there weren't no blacks working in none of these places.

Our first bank was the Drexel Bank, it was at Cottage Grove and Oakwood Boulevard, and we succeeded in getting a black there. One of the members of my church had a bottling beverage distributing company in the black community; we had the picket line around and I asked him not to go in. He spit in my face and he went in. But we won. The first meeting I had with them, they told me no way were they going to hire any blacks. I told them, you don't hire none, we're going to put a picket line. We kept the picket line and finally the first black was hired. Then we went to march on a bank at 47th and Cottage Grove. They hired some blacks. Then the word spread to downtown to the banks, and the banks downtown started, because we started passing out leaflets all up and down State Street.

Not a department store in State Street had a black salesperson in it, not one. And we started leafleting down there, and finally they started hiring blacks as salespersons. We brought about a black awareness to what we were doing over the entire black community. You had an informed black public. We brought about a new awareness.

Back in the fifties the furthest south that a black could live was 63rd Street. Blacks moved to 67th, and white people started burning and everything else. There was a Catholic church that was the headquarters of the white movement to keep Negroes out of Park Manor. When blacks moved over there, whites started rebelling. In the Packinghouse union, I kept on arguing I ought to do something. They finally agreed, and I had a committee to work with: Sidney Williams, who was then head of the Urban League; Robert Landrum, a real estate man; a gentleman by the name of Vernon Jarrett; and Horace Cayton, an old Socialist, used to be head of the Parkway Community House. We led the crusade.

We protested and fought; we had rallies. We marched downtown and passed out leaflets for blacks to live in these different places. We got black and white people, packinghouse workers, we got white communities activists. Basically most of them came from the unions. Most of them would be trade union leaders and trade union workers, members of the unions. I got a lot of support from the black packinghouse workers, some few white packinghouse workers, from members of the UE [United Electrical Workers] union, from the Mine and Smelter Workers union, from the Farm Equipment Workers union. From all of the left unions I got support, black and white. It wasn't just black. Black and white, and we were a meaningful force.

In the 1950s the interracial unity that characterized the organizing era faltered as black union activism around civil rights issues clashed with the sensibilities of many white UPWA members. Francis Connell, a mechanic at Swift, voiced the sentiments of many whites, stating "as far as discrimination is concerned, the union should do all it can within the plant. They should confine it to that. When they talk about discrimination outside, housing, etc., that has nothing to do with the union."7

Black insurgency accentuated fragmentary tendencies that had reasserted themselves within the union. The new dynamic had received symbolic expression in 1949 when the Chicago District moved its headquarters from Back-of-the-Yards into a black neighborhood. Herb March felt that the relocation led to a slackening of white involvement. "Whites were all for the union," he noted, "but they didn't feel comfortable going over at night into the black community for meetings." Even as staunch a unionist as Gertie Kamarczyk stopped attending union functions. "It was too much of the colored's concern," she reasoned. "I didn't think they really wanted me there, so I just didn't go after a while."[8]

Charles Hayes recalled that at the time the decision to move the headquarters was controversial. "We were criticized for that," he remembered. "Some of the leaders thought it was wrong to leave. We were moving farther away from the stockyards, but we were also moving closer to where the bulk of our members were." Although not all unionists agreed with Sam Parks that white participation was in decline prior to the move, the relocation further widened the gulf between black activists and white leftist leaders.

Sam Parks

The union hall was sitting at 48th and Marshfield, all-Polish neighborhood. 49th and Wabash was where the International Workers Order [IWO] had its headquarters at Bacon's Casino. The executive secretary of that fraternal order was a woman by the name of Louise Patterson. Her husband was a lawyer by the name of William Patterson, a member of the National Committee of the Communist Party. She met me one night and she said, "Sam, we're about to lose this building." So I came up with the idea first to buy the IWO headquarters. Herb fought it. Herb March had a program going, wants to buy a building down at 45th and Ashland, still in the same white Polish neighborhood. Helstein fought it; other left whites fought it. [District Director Harold Nielsen] bought it, and the reason that he bought it was because he could see that every meeting you call at 48th and Marshfield, in the white community, the union hall is full of nothing but black members, there wasn't no whites there. So if you moved over to 49th and Wabash, it ain't going to change nothing anyway. You still got blacks attending, and then you're one block from the police station over there, because the district police station used to be at 48th and Wabash. And my program was if whites can come to 48th and Marshfield, where there ain't no police station, surely whites can come to 49th and Wabash, where there is one. And I started to campaign, with Nielsen's support, and the district overwhelmingly voted to buy that building.

By the middle of the 1950s, it was clear that the meatpacking industry was changing. The packers began to phase out their urban operations and relocate in the rural hinterlands. Plant closings decimated the membership of the Chicago UPWA. Wilson led the exodus from the Chicago stockyards, eliminating its killing operations in 1955 and shutting the entire plant two years later. Armour followed in 1959, and Swift closed its doors in the early 1960s.

The demise of the stockyards destroyed the social base for activism within the union as workers struggled with layoffs, retraining, and redundancies. Nevertheless, at the leadership level, UPWA officials continued to play a role in the unfolding civil rights movement. Charles Hayes, for instance, lent crucial support when King came north in 1966.

Charles Hayes

In the late fifties, Martin Luther King came along, and after they had the Montgomery Bus Boycott some of us from our union went to the South and joined hands with that movement down there. When other unions were remaining aloof from that movement, our union raised some $11,000 from

Soldier Field rally in 1966, where Martin Luther King Jr. announced his plans to force the City of Chicago to open housing in white neighborhoods to blacks. King and Coretta Scott King are under the umbrella; UPWA President Ralph Helstein is third from the right. *Used with permission of the State Historical Society of Wisconsin [WHi (X3) 50374].*

its own members, white and black, and we took it in a check and presented it to Martin Luther King and the Southern Christian Leadership Conference. I participated and attended the first organizational meeting of the Southern Christian Leadership Conference at King's daddy's church in Atlanta, Georgia.

Even when King came to Chicago, I was the only union person who served as a part of that committee. I remember the UAW were one of the more progressive unions who would not get on the side of King—nor would they get on the side of Richard Daley and the city forces who were trying to keep the neighborhoods as they were. The UAW had a table sitting in the middle.

Although no longer packinghouse workers, many former UPWA members retained an activist orientation. Schooled in the UPWA's confrontational style, they carried the struggle into other unions and other organizations. Several former UPWA stalwarts played key visible roles in the Chicago mayoral campaign of Harold Washington. Thousands, of course, never again were organizationally active, but out of their union experience they carried with them a commitment to equality and racial justice that shaped their subsequent behavior and personal lives.

Sam Parks

During all of this I came to learn one thing, and that is that no one man has the answer within himself to the problems of humanity, no one man. It takes a collective. I learned another thing that's very, very basic, and that is that one must have contentment, individual, inside contentment, and satisfaction in order to make your major contribution. You can't have contradictions eating your ass up inside, and you're going to get out there and lead a bunch of people and help them to get somewhere.

All in all, I think the years that I spent in the packing union, the years that I spent working with the Communists, working with the Progressives and everything else, I think it helped to build me into a better man than what I was when I started out. I was taught lessons. And a lot of stuff I learned, I make applicable today in the work I'm doing politically in the Democratic Party. I work to build a strong organization in my ward organization. And I hope someday that the Democratic Party will return to the principles of Franklin Delano Roosevelt—that man was a great president because he had the Left and everything working with him. They didn't dominate, but they were working. And I think the philosophy and programs of the Democratic Party is for the best interests of the black people and for the working people, and I think it needs to be resurrected in the spirit that was there.

Philip Weightman

I would hope that the collective experiences that I have had and others have had has contributed to the advancement of the welfare and the growth of the packinghouse workers' right to participate in the fullness of American life.

I got a great deal of experience in dealing with people, how to treat people. How to listen and understand them, and to recognize the sufferings of people. And I have learned to be compassionate. I listen. Because in hearing the cries and the problems of people, I recognize what my duty still is as long as I live: to do what I can to be helpful.

3

"IT WAS THE ONLY WAY TO GET THE JOB DONE"
Unionism and Race Relations in Kansas City

When blues musicians sang "Going to Kansas City" in the 1920s and 1930s, it was very likely that packinghouse workers were among the most important patrons of the celebrated interwar African American culture of that city. Indeed, blacks had deeper roots in the local meatpacking industry than in any other metropolitan area. While most African Americans obtained a permanent foothold in meatpacking only during World War I, Kansas City blacks had established a solid presence in that industry during the late nineteenth century. In 1879, hundreds of ex-slaves fleeing the restoration of white rule in the South found work at the understaffed Armour plant. Their numbers grew steadily to 2,000 in 1920, including 250 black women. Packinghouses operated by all Big Four firms, and several smaller concerns, made Kansas City the nation's second-largest meatpacking center in the 1930s.

While packinghouse work was hard, disagreeable, and irregular, the availability of jobs and relatively high pay made it a desirable occupation within Kansas City's black working class. The willingness of meatpacking firms to hire blacks contrasted sharply with employment practices elsewhere in Kansas City; in 1929, only one-quarter of the businesses in greater Kansas City employed blacks at all. Only small numbers of professionals, store owners, Pullman porters, restaurant waiters, and teamsters earned more than packinghouse workers.

Outside the packinghouses, black workers encountered rigid residential and social segregation. Segregation of neighborhoods, schools, services, and recreation sharply demarcated the separate world of Kansas City's blacks. Restrictive covenants sought to maintain residential segregation as the black population grew in the 1910s and 1920s, and "improvement" associations kept their areas "white territory" by resorting to intimidation and violence if legal methods failed. When blacks overcame resistance and successfully purchased houses on previously lily-white blocks, white homeowners quickly fled to new subdivisions.

The expansion of popular culture in the 1920s and 1930s generally reinforced Kansas City's color line. Blacks and whites usually enjoyed leisure and recreation in racially defined arenas, aside from occasional interracial contact when whites attended black events. Barnstorming black jazz musicians, such as Benny Moten and Count Basie, made Kansas City a center for the creative energies of swing orchestras. But downtown jazz clubs admitted only white customers; black music enthusiasts attended the nightclubs lining Twelfth and Eighteenth Streets. Black baseball fans went to see luminaries such as Satchel Paige play for the Kansas City Monarchs (the dominant team in the National Negro League), while whites watched future stars Mickey Mantle and Yogi Berra perform for the Kansas City Blues, a minor league team owned by the New York Yankees. Blacks were not admitted to bowling alleys, skating rinks, and amusement parks and were denied access to all public and private swimming pools. Downtown department stores sold goods to blacks but would not let them try clothes on, eat at in-house restaurants, or work as clerks. Strict racial separation extended to movie theaters, the school system, hospitals, churches, hotels, and even the Girl Scouts and the Boy Scouts.

Discrimination inadvertently encouraged the development of a rich and race-conscious black society in Kansas City. A thick web of community institutions produced a flourishing black culture, nurtured by a segregated economy and funded by the wages of thousands of working-class blacks. Blacks built their own hotels and hospitals and organized an informal network of rooming houses and restaurants in the homes of black families to counteract exclusion from the white establishments. The *Kansas City Call* served as the voice of the community on both the Missouri and Kansas sides of the river, and heavily attended Baptist, Methodist, and evangelical churches provided spiritual solace and organizational common ground. Blacks formed protective associations to defend their homes against harassment and bombings, and huge crowds attended rallies featuring Marcus Garvey in 1922.

Kansas City's separate black society represented both an opportunity and a challenge to union organizers. Scorned by most whites, Kansas City blacks constituted a cohesive community that could be a force to aid or undermine any effort to organize the packinghouses.

The pivotal campaign in the Kansas City packinghouse district took place at the Armour plant. A determined organizing drive initiated by Charles R. Fischer and a small group of Socialists established important beachheads of support among black and Croatian workers by 1937. A four-day plant occupation in 1938 cemented the union's interracial alliance and led to the organization of other plants in the Kansas City area. By the end of World War II, the local unions had established a solid tradition of involving both blacks and whites in leadership positions. This was especially true in the Armour plant, where a mixture of white ethnics and blacks of both sexes divided important union posts.

In the 1950s, the UPWA locals became important participants in the civil rights protests that engulfed Kansas City and broke down the informal Jim Crow practices that had characterized urban race relations for more than a half-century. But unlike Chicago and Waterloo, Kansas City locals were primarily supporters of civil rights activities initiated by other groups, rather than leaders in their own right. Nonetheless, their participation was crucial because of the organizational and material resources of the UPWA locals and the influence of packinghouse workers in churches and civil rights groups such as the NAACP. As in other meatpacking centers, Kansas City's UPWA members provided a rank-and-file link between labor and the emerging civil rights movement.

William Raspberry

William Raspberry was a perceptive observer of black life in Kansas City and of how unions contributed to enormous changes in the course of his life. He combined admiration for Booker T. Washington's philosophy of individual uplift with a firm commitment to the principles of collective action and a stringent critique of the manner in which racism affected the everyday experiences of Kansas City's black community.

Raspberry was born in 1911 in Mississippi. His family moved to St. Louis in 1913 and then to Kansas City in 1924. Raspberry moved around Missouri and worked at a number of different jobs before getting hired at the Meyer Kornblum packinghouse in 1942. Soon afterward, the Campbell Soup Company purchased the Kornblum plant and rechristened it the Central Packing Company. Raspberry joined UPWA Local 36 and quickly became active in the union, serving on the bargaining and grievance committees for most of his stay in the plant. He also served as the financial secretary, vice president, and president of the local, as well as representing it at numerous UPWA conventions and conferences and in the Greater Kansas City Industrial Union Council. When Central Packing closed in 1961, Raspberry found employment at the Wilson plant in Kansas City and was elected the president of UPWA Local 20 in 1965. He retired when the Wilson plant closed in 1975.[1]

I was born in Mississippi, and my grandfather had land down there. My father kind of loafed around and on Monday mornings, the plantation owner didn't want to see no black guy riding around or walking around or anything. Wanted to see him working on Monday morning. So this guy struck my father, and said "I don't want you riding around my folks, my niggers, because you're no good influence on them." After the second time and third time this guy cussed him, my dad said he pulled him off the horse and roughed him up and got back on his horse and rode on and kept on riding. So he didn't get back [home], so he got tied up with a guy over at the lumber company. He learned pretty quick what there was to be learned about lumber and how to make a tree fall without busting it up, and he got to where he could tell just about how many board feet was in a tree. This is down in Arkansas and southeastern Missouri. When the war was over he kept working for him, until the twenties and I guess things got kind of bad. That's when we moved to St. Louis. He worked in the lumberyards there for a while, then he went to work for the packinghouse. He was a beef lugger there. I guess that sort of steered me to the packinghouse business, because he was doing pretty good.

My father took Booker Washington's advice, he said, "if you dig down where you are, you'll come up with something sooner or later." My father figured he could make it anywhere at any time, because if there was a job to be done, he was going to do it and do it well. He saw to instill in us too, if you were going to do something, be on time, stay until it's done, and make sure you did what you could.

My mother was an unusual woman. She did a lot of Bible reading, and the Bible is one book that says, you know, you supposed to be fair with everybody and do justice to all things.

My folks said that the blacks could do the dirty work but they couldn't get into the union, or if they got into the union they would be in the union for the laborers. At the time the skilled [workers] got what they wanted, they just left the black laborers hanging out there. So that's about all I knew about it at that time, which was enough to turn me off.

The International [Industrial] Workers of the World had at one time tried to organize everyone in an industrial union, and he liked that idea, but that didn't last. And then the A.F. of L. was a craft union, and they organized on the principle of craft. So, he didn't appreciate them.

The packinghouse workers had in '21 a big organizing effort. But the organizers had blacks in auxiliaries or semiskilled groups. We were living in St. Louis then. My father didn't think too much of the unions because if the whites got what they wanted they would start negotiating for the blacks.

The guys got back together and went back to work, they broke the strike. And I remember that was years later, we used to go up to white brothers and say, if you don't let us in your union, we'll break your strike. It was one of the weapons we had that we could use.

Raspberry vividly recalled how race infiltrated all aspects of social relations in Kansas City.

It was almost like two different countries. The only thing that wasn't segregated to my knowledge was the streetcars. But you wouldn't go down to sit down beside some white person because they would probably get up. Yes,

Kansas City was pretty bad. You was just black, and that was it. I mean they didn't call us black then. [laughs]

In the twenties, if you go to look for a job, they would say, "We don't have no job today, boy." That was it. Steel, they had common laborers mostly, the railroad jobs, and packinghouses. Auto used them in custodial. No assembly lines. It was so deeply embedded it was hard to uproot.

One Sunday morning, my uncle and I rolled up the 2500 block, he and I were going to church that morning. He wanted to see somebody he knew. This realtor came up and told my uncle he wanted to talk to him. So, uncle said, sure we can talk, of course, he never did like him too much 'cause he knew he was a racist. So, he said, "Well, I just wanted to warn you. I don't want you selling no houses on this block, I don't want you showing no houses on this block, don't get it in your head that you're going to show houses in this block, 'cause if you do, if you move somebody in here, we're going to bomb your black eyes out." So my uncle sat for a minute, he said, "Well, that means I'll have to start making bombs again. 'Cause if anybody throw a bomb at me, I'm going to throw one back at him." And he drove off, and that was the end of that, at least as far as I know. But when we first moved up there, we heard a noise outside, I had a shotgun and he had a pistol. We'd get up and be ready for whatever happened. They set a small fire outside one of the houses, but that was the only thing to happen.

No matter what your position was in the community, when you got out of the community you just had a black face. I remember one Sunday morning I took my brother out to 55th and Oak, and I was sitting out in the car, and he went in. It was a drugstore he worked at. While I was sitting there I saw this cop go past the drugstore, go down the street and turn around and come back and said, "What're you doing here?" I said, "I'm waiting for my brother." "Where is he?" I said, "He's in the drugstore." He said, "Get out, get out of your car and open the trunk."

I had been painting, and I had a crowbar, and all my painting things—my brushes, my buckets, my drop cloths—and all that made a difference was my hammer and a crowbar. So he said, "What're you doing with this hammer and a crowbar?" So I told him. He said, "You say you've got a brother in there?" I got mad, but what could you do, you have to go along, man, so I said, "Yeah." So he went in there and brought me over and said, "Do you know this boy? Do any of you know this boy?" And I'm about forty years old, thirty-five years old. My brother and the manager walked out then, and he said, "Hi, Ras." I said, "Hi, there." And the cop said, "So you know him?" and he said, "Sure, I know him." He said, "OK," and he walked out. No apologies or nothing to me. So, it leaves a little scar. But, you've already gotten pretty tough by now, you can take a lot of stuff.

Kansas City was supposed to have been the jazz mecca, and we did have some good people here. You go there sometimes stay there until two or three o'clock in the morning, you know you got to go to work the next day. Then they had Blue Mondays, and Mondays, that was all day, they jammed all day long on Mondays for a while. One group would come in and leave, and another would take his place, and it'd just go on and on. And also the whites who came to town, although the blacks couldn't go downtown to wherever they were playing, they would come out here and sit in with the guys and blow. See, people in the arts were the people who really started the race relation thing going.

You also had a lot of baseball players moving through here because you had the Kansas City Monarchs. It was the biggest thing in town as far as sports was concerned, 'cause there was no black basketball players, there was no black players in any other national sports. And the Monarchs were better at the time than the Blues, which was the white team. That stadium was about 15, maybe 20,000 max. They'd fill it up. There'd be a lot of whites out there to see them play, too.

Every time a team would come to play them they had to have a place to stay. Musicians would come in town and they would stop in a home because they couldn't get no hotels. And there were a few other people who traveled, and when they hit the town they wanted room and board, and they'd want some home. It was a way of life. Once in a while they'd invite some friends over to have dinner and meet these celebrities. Like Sidney Poitier, I met him. I met a lot of people like that. All the entertainers and musicians when they came to town they had to live in somebody's home.

Raspberry worked in a series of jobs in the 1920s. In 1928 he roomed in a house located in a middle-class black neighborhood that whites recently had vacated. The respectable lifestyle of a calf skinner who lived nearby left a lasting impression.

Most people had roomers, then. One house I lived in on 25th and Brooklyn, this woman had about three rooms rented to railroad men, and their wives was living here regularly, and whenever they was in town at all, then they'd be there.

In 1928 I met this guy who was a packinghouse worker who lived on the same block that I lived on, and all these blacks had moved in 1928. They were teachers and a couple of doctors and railroad people, dining-car waiters or chef cooks, Pullman porters. He impressed me more than some of the doctors because he was clean, he was dressed nice, and he was the first guy I'd seen growing Bermuda grass in this section of the country. He had a neatly manicured lawn, and his wife kept flowers around it, and he kept his house painted as was necessary. I got to know him, and I said, "What do you do?" And he said he worked at the packinghouse.

In the meantime I had read this article in the *Readers Digest* that said there was more black guys with degrees working at Union Station as redcaps than there was in any other institution in the world. There was only about three doctors in this town that you could look up to as being good fellows. You looked up to them because they had degrees and all, but they didn't show you too much. If you were a dentist, he was probably out waiting tables at the country club or be on the road as a Pullman porter. You had to wait until he came back to his office to open up, then you'd go down and get a tooth pulled.

When I was in school, I took more trades than I did the others. And that had been a debate, I remember W. E. B. Du Bois versus Booker T. Washington. Du Bois was preaching that blacks should get educated and become lawyers and doctors. So, Washington said train your hands and mind, you get enough of everything. You've got to have enough math, enough English. You've got to be able to communicate, and you have to be able to figure out your job if you get a job. But he said it was the trade that blacks should have gotten into. And I saw the wisdom in that. See, for a long time in the packinghouse I was making more money than most professionals.

In the 1930s, Raspberry participated in the black community's intellectual ferment and took his first steps toward overcoming enmity between the races. He closely followed the early development of the CIO and its effort to implement egalitarian racial policies.

I went to church, and we did a lot of studying. Then, in the thirties, everybody started reading and that was the beginning of the intellectual age, more books was being published and everybody was reading. Then there was the streetcar, and it took a little longer to get to work then than it does now. So you sat and you read a couple of chapters going to and from work. If you read something somebody else was reading, you'd discuss it with them. There seemed to be a craving for knowledge and information during that period. Every time there's a big crisis, people seem to start seeking.

A lot of women had clubs. They'd play cards during their meetings, and they'd discuss these things, and you could go to churches and other organizations and these social groups. There were twenty-five or thirty women at them, and some belonged to more than one group. They'd meet in their homes and other places, wherever necessary. They'd have teas to raise money and do other things. 'Cause during that time a lot of guys had rent raising parties, once a month they'd have a party and pay their rent. And some of them were successful at it. And you went to those places and it was almost like being at church, everybody was friendly.

We read just about everything, anything that was published at that time, there'd be somebody who'd read it. Richard Wright was one of the books that was discussed often, and when *Strange Fruit* came out, that was another one. Whatever even made some reference to progress for black folks, we had to have it to see if it was for us or against us. [laughs]

We also had what they called race relations. Instead of our civil rights, it was called race relations. A group from Park College and other people from

Kansas City who was white would meet at the YMCA on Tuesdays and discuss the problems. Just simple communication, saying "hello" to you without being offensive.

One white woman gave me *Native Son,* she wanted to know, "Well, are white folks really as bad as Mr. Wright portrayed them as being to the blacks?" I said, he might have exaggerated some parts, to make the book sell, but basically he wrote the truth.

This was a time that the races were beginning to get together and discuss this imaginary thing that existed between us. So, it was started. That first step is the beginning of unity, so it was slow, but we were stepping. We were having meetings, interracial meetings, and the police would come in and break them up at that time. Whites and blacks were not supposed to congregate together at that time. It was almost like a secret organization, you have to meet underground, but the police department used to be kind of rough.

It was about '35 I guess, when they first started to try and organize unions. When the union first started, I was sort of skeptical of them. Then I got started reading about the CIO, what their program was, and I knew some of the guys working at the packinghouse, and I got to talking to them. After the CIO came in I kind of liked the idea. Equality of man. The CIO came along and said well, if you get on a job, from the day you're hired, your seniority starts. And whoever comes behind you, gets behind you. Color has nothing to do with it. Religion has nothing to do with it. And there would be no more, what you call "half-pint" for the boss. If you work, no matter what color you are, irregardless of race, creed, or color, you had a right to work, and you had a right to earn a decent living. It was an organization I could get in, and I won't be the last one hired and the first one fired. I was impressed, and I kept up with them.

I remember when Armour had a sit-in strike over there. They stayed in the plant until they got some type of an agreement. They shut them down pretty good.

I kept up with it; I knew some of the fellows and I knew what was going on. Of course, everybody wasn't for it, but the masses were. They had an experience of what the strike did. They knew that if they could get an organization that was going to protect them as well as the other man, it was an advantage to them.

Charles R. Fischer

Charles R. Fischer was born in 1907 in Springhill, Pennsylvania, of Dutch ancestry. His father was an active member of the International Association of Machinists. Fischer first worked in the press room of the Kansas City Star *in the 1920s and in 1929 was hired in the powerhouse of the Armour plant. In the 1930s he was a member of the Socialist Party and ran for office on its ticket in 1938. Fischer was a key figure in the small group of packinghouse workers who initiated the successful organizing drive in the late 1930s, and he remained a leader of the local union until 1966. He was an active participant in the union's four-day occupation of the Armour plant in 1938, which was sparked by a dispute involving four blacks and one Croatian.*

There were five guys far down in the hide cellar, fired unjustly. OK, so the word got around we're going to have a sit-down strike, and we took that plant over for five days. We got that after the Automobile Workers who had sit-down strike after sit-down strike and forced them into submission on a production line there. They were forced to negotiate whether they liked it or not. And as a result of that, we signed up hundreds and hundreds and hundreds of people. We had our headquarters in the lard house, and we had all these people come in and sign up. And that was really the time that got the majority signed up in the organization.

The sit-in was carefully organized. Elected committees kept the plant clean, obtained food from supporters outside the plant, and performed other duties. The union relieved the tedium of the strike by organizing social activities, which reinforced the interracial aspect of the sit-down experience.

Oh they played cards, they sang union songs. And then we had some very good musicians that could play guitar, and they could play, like sax, and trombone, trumpet; you name it, we had it in there. Of course we didn't have any piano to play—it would be nice if we did! But it was entertainment. And then there were several guys who had very good voices, there were several baritones in there among the black guys. They were fabulous, fabulous. We had one Irish tenor there that, he could sing Irish songs to you all day long! He was great. Yes, he was great.

Old Jim Lumpkin composed these things. I can remember a few of the words of one of them that went something like this: "We're the CIO, just watch us go. Don't care about ice, don't care about snow." Songs like that, you know. But I can't recall the words or any of the others. He was quite a guy, he composed a whole bunch of songs, a whole bunch of songs that were sung during that strike. He didn't compose that one for us, but nevertheless it was one of the songs that we sang.

Those people were convinced that we were right, and we were going to see it out, and we did. So, after the majority decided that we would hold out to the end, why we had it made, we had it made then. But we turned out on top on that.

Then the word got around the plants around the circuit, it caught like wildfire then, it caught like wildfire. Oh I'm talking about like St. Joe and Omaha, St. Louis, Chicago, Fort Worth, Oklahoma City, Denver, Atlanta, Birmingham, you name it.

Fischer credited the strike with establishing a solid interracial alliance inside the Armour local and contributing to the UPWA's firm stand against racism.

It left a unity, a friendship there that couldn't have been created in any other way. It forged that final bond between all of the races, between the religions and every phase of social life. It did the job that we couldn't have done otherwise; it really got the job done. After that sit-down strike there was never any division whatsoever as far as tension between the races was concerned. We had none, from then on. It really accomplished a purpose.

When they saw that we were going to be a union who would absolutely not tolerate prejudiced tendencies, absolutely no prejudicial actions whatsoever, that's what sold them. It wasn't because it was CIO. It wasn't because it was anti–A.F. of L. It was because of the basic policy of the PWOC at the time. And then when the United Packinghouse Workers came into being, it was a part of the constitution and a part of all the contracts that were negotiated that there would be absolutely no discrimination. And we meant what we said.

William Raspberry

The success of the Armour strike, and his subsequent experience with the union's interracial policies, made Raspberry an enthusiastic and active member of the UPWA and the CIO. He combined a belief that mutual material interests underlay white-black cooperation with openness to dissident points of view.

The CIO policies were carried out strictly in the PWOC. You had as many blacks on the committees and officers as you had whites. The policy of the CIO was carried out that there should be no discrimination because of race, creed, or color, and seniority shall be the governing factor.

It was pretty integrated, because whites saw advantages in it, because there were certain things they had been trying to get for themselves, and they wasn't able to get it. They figured that it was to their mutual benefit to get along.

We always said, if the company is willing to pay you, a white man, a nickel more than he's paying a black man, you're not getting enough either. Just the fact that I can separate you by saying, "Hey, I'm going to give you a nickel an hour more than I'm giving him," is blinding this guy to the fact that he's not getting paid what he's worth in the first place. So in order to get what you're worth, you've got to cut out that nickel an hour more and let everybody get what he's worth. But you're going to have a division if one group is getting a nickel an hour more than the other. So just to work together you cut that nickel out and let everybody make a living. What we were trying to do is get more money for everybody. We fought that hard, and in an international convention most of our time was spent trying to convince people that you have to work together, not as individuals, collectively, and it was the only way to get the job done. It changes them.

We spent as much time in the conventions on the racial things than we did on anything else. We had a lot of good white folks in there fighting, too. Of course a lot of people said that they were Communists, and there were some Communists in it, there is no question about it, there were Communists in it, but they weren't in the top office.

There was one boy in particular, Gordon Monroe, they used to call him a Commie. I liked him, he was a good guy. I used to go over to his house and we would sit down and talk. I liked Gordon because Gordon was a good person, and his politics didn't affect me one way or the other. I used to go out to his house and he would come to ours, and we would sit down and visit. Some of the guys used to come around and try to interest me in the Communist Party. I said, "If we work hard enough here, we will get the consideration that we need." I didn't think the Communists were any different people than anybody else; I didn't think they had any special ties to racial equality or things like that.

I used to take the *Daily Worker,* and I would read it, because I used to take a lot of stuff. Anything that came along that was different, I wanted to know about it. They sold it on the street. And once in a while somebody would bring one into the plant, and I think that there was a few white Communists in there. See, there were a lot of socialists among the Croatians and the Slovakians, and the Lithuanians. Because they had been oppressed, and they developed a different philosophy. They knew that the capitalist system was oppressive to the poor. I didn't say white or black, I say oppressive to the poor. So they knew that, and they were looking for a better way out then, before some of them came over here.

I did some research on the Communist Party. If the Communist Party was ever perfected, it would be ideal. But there's no incentive. Most people would drag their feet unless they're getting something out of it, so that's all the bad part about it. Matter of fact the capitalist system is not perfect, and I think it's just about on its way out; I think it's served its purpose. I don't know what's going to take its place.

Virginia Houston

Employment in meatpacking also served as a means of upward mobility for black women like Virginia Houston. Born in Pine Bluff, Arkansas, in 1918, Houston moved to Kansas City in 1934 with her husband. She worked at a variety of domestic and restaurant jobs in the 1930s before obtaining employment at the Sunflower Munitions plant at the beginning of World War II. When that plant closed at the end of the war, she was able to get hired into the hog offal department of the Armour packinghouse. She became a departmental steward after participat-

ing in the 1948 strike and served on several leadership committees of Local 15. When the plant closed in 1965, Houston worked at the Lake City Munitions plant for four years, was out of work for one year, and then found a job at the Lipton Tea plant. She became active in Teamsters Local 838 at the Lipton plant and stayed there until retiring in 1985.[2]

I never have been fired off of a job in my life, because I was raised in the South—Arkansas was my home—and I didn't know nothin' 'bout nothing BUT work. Work didn't bother me. My grandmother and grandfather raised me because my mother and daddy died when I was small. They rented land, they was sharecroppers. I done everything on the farm—chopped cotton, cleaned corn, stripped sorghum meat. We had horses and cows and mules and chickens and turkeys and geese. That belonged to us, but the land didn't.

In 1934 I came to Kansas City. A lot of my younger cousins and relatives was here, and we kept in touch. They would write to me all the time and tell me about the opportunities they had here, and why didn't I come on up here where I could get me a job and where I could learn something beside being on that farm. Well, naturally I was young and I took their advice and came on up here.

When I first came to Kansas City, racism was really something. There was a whole lot of places black people couldn't go. You wasn't allowed to go in a lot of restaurants. There was only three theaters that the black people could go to. You could sit anywhere because didn't nobody go there but black people. You couldn't go downtown to any of those white restaurants and eat there. You had to go down and eat on 12th Street, or you ate on 18th Street, or you ate at home.

When I first came here, you could always go out to Swope Park. That's the great big park with the zoo. But you had a certain place where you had your picnic. You could go in the zoo and look at the animals, they didn't bother you for that. But other than that, you just couldn't do it. Fairlane Park, the only time black folk could go out there would be the last day of the season, when they got ready to close it down. But other than that, you couldn't go all through the summer, kids or nobody. And they had all them rides, you know, the Big Dipper and the ups and downs and the merry-go-rounds. You couldn't go in no swimming pools unless you had one of your own. But didn't nobody have one 'cause they wasn't able. I never did learn how to swim. All the swimming pools was private, you couldn't go to them. And those out there at Swope Park, you wasn't allow to go in.

I done some of all kind of work since I came here in 1934. I worked in private families, I worked for doctors and lawyers and packinghouse and Sunflower Ordnance during the war, Lake City during the war, and ended up at Lipton Tea. Things are so much different now than they was then, because when I first come here you couldn't get a factory job. After it got so where you could get factory jobs, well I went to Sunflower Ordnance. When

Sunflower Ordnance closed down in V-J Day or V-D Day or whatever day it was, then I was out of work.

But I knew a lot of people that worked for Armour and Company. I went down there for a whole week before I got hired. Those packinghouse jobs at that particular time was the best job that you could get where you could be making any kind of money. And I stayed there for nineteen and a half years, 'til Armour's got ready to move out of town.

At Armour, Houston was hired into the hog offal department. She recalled the employment manager warning her that when she reported for work the first day, "you have you on some boots and bring you some old clothes to work in that you don't care nothing about because this is a pretty nasty place where you're going to be working." The union had a strong presence in this department.

Yeah, it was terrible. [laughs] But that was a dirty job! We was cleanin' them hog guts, that what we was doing. They had those guys up there on the head table, they was the ones putting them down a chute down to the girls on the floor and then you take one of them—you'd have to have a knife and a steel—and punch a hole in it and slide it on that rod. This rod it got holes up on here and that water would be comin' down in that. Then you just do that until you get that whole thing on that rod and get it all clean. Then you cut 'em off and you'd put 'em in the buckets. They'd have that man that came down there and pour 'em in that tub where those ladies was, giving them the finishin' touches. Then later on, when they modernized it some, they put a trough up. Well, that eliminated that man 'cause we'd have to do it. Then when you cut 'em off, all you had to do was go and put them in that trough and they slide on down.

When I started there in the hog offal it wasn't nothing in there but black women. But later on they hired one or two white women, but most of the women in the offal had a lot of seniority. The other new departments that they added on to there, well they had a lot of white women in there 'cause they added on the canned meats and frozen food. Well they was hiring a lot of people over there because they was packaging it over there. But the most of the women in the offal had a lot of seniority so we never did get too many new people. Some of them women when I went down there had been there fifteen and twenty years.

Dora Vaughn was a steward in offal. Every time somebody new come in there she'd always go to 'em and talk to 'em and tell 'em what the union consist of. She would bring us our union card and say, "Now you a union member and if you have any problems or any trouble, you come to me. Tell the foreman you want to see your steward and he'll excuse you and let you come to me or just tell him to tell me you want to see me." She says, "Best for you to tell him that you want to see me and when he come to me then I can come and find out what your problem is." So that's the way I first got into it.

If they had a problem, she'd come up there and tell that foreman that he had to put somebody in her place and then they would go out. Then if they didn't get it settled down there just by talking—that would be the first step. See you talk it out in the first step and you didn't get it settled then you'd put it in writing which would be in the second step. If they didn't get it settled up then they would send it on up to the third step and that's when Jesse Prosten, the boys from Chicago would come in to try to get it settled.

The UPWA's 1948 strike proved a turning point for Virginia Houston's partici-pation in the Armour union. Soon after the strike ended, she took Dora Vaughn's place as departmental steward. By the 1950s, she was one of the most important black women leaders of the local union.

I wasn't real active in the union then. That made me mad because they offered us nine cents before we went out of there and we went out of there and walked up and down that picket line. And then we finally went right back in there for the same nine cents. See that was just purely foolish. A lot of them people had house payments and things to make and they had their family and had children going to school and kids and things and they couldn't afford to stay out of there all them months like they did. A lot of them crossed the picket line and went back in there and that's what broke the strike. At first it was kind of rough on them. They was throwing cocktail bombs in people houses and putting sugar in their gas tanks and throwing bricks through people's windows.

That '48 strike was something else. There was a long time before they got over that strike. A lot of people was mad when they went back in there because a lot of them people crossed the picket line went back in there. They walked around there for about a week or two weeks and wouldn't have noth-ing to say to each other. Finally they got just back like they was, where every-body got friendly and everything and, you know, forgot all about it. It was what really made me take more active in the union.

The lady that had the job, she had gotten to the place that she was getting up in age, and she wanted to give it up. And then, I would attend all the union meetings, and whenever something would come up on the floor, well I would get up and speak my opinion about it. After I got to be a steward in my department, I carried myself out good.

If you done good on your job, and stood up for your rights on your job, then they would hold an election. That's the way you got elected to the union. If you would speak up for yourself and speak up for your rights, well, they would nominate that person to be a steward, or be on the execu-tive board or on the bargaining committee, or something like that. That's the way I got active in the union. 'Cause I always have spoken for my rights, you know.

You have to know how to try to get along with people. Because you can't go in there with an attitude just because you elected to be something you can dominate people and tell people what they can do and what they can't do. You have to know how to talk to people. You have to try to get the respect of the people, and then you have to try to treat them so they will respect you. You have to try to carry yourself in a way so people will respect you, and listen to what you've got to say.

As in many UPWA plants, the Armour local employed stoppages and slowdowns in conjunction with more routine reliance on negotiations and the grievance procedure.

Every once in a while they would do it, they would carry it that far. Most of the time when they would do that is contract negotiations. They didn't do it to make it so obvious, but it would be made obvious. The company knew what they was doing and they knew what they was doing too. [laughs] But nobody never did get fired. Not in my department. I didn't know anything about it. After I got to be a steward, nobody never did.

We always took our orders from the higher-ups. We didn't just go to work and do something on our own 'cause we wasn't allowed to, you know, union-wise. If they hit a snag in Chicago, then that negotiating committee would call back and give Tony [Kostelac, the local union's secretary-treasurer] the word, which Ralph Helstein would be done already give him up there in Chicago. Then Tony would call them stewards out there from every department, and tell that what that negotiating committee had told him and go back in there and tell those people what to do, don't do no more and no less.

Houston and other black women active in the union also were very involved in their churches. Houston saw similar motivations behind these two spheres of activity.

I'm an usher in my church, I've always been an usher, I've liked that. I joined the church when I was nine years old in Arkansas, and I been ushing ever since. I ushered at St. Stephen Baptist Church, and I'm usher out here to Zion Grove Missionary Baptist Church. I belonged to the senior usher board, and I've been on different boards and different auxiliaries.

I was active in the church before I went to the packinghouse, 'cause I was brought up in the church in the country. After I got out of the union, there wasn't nothing for me to do but fall back to being more active then in the church than I was before. Because a lot of time the union would take up a lot of my time, something would be going on in the church that I couldn't participate in. But after that shipped out, well then I had more time to participate in my next best activity.

79

Some of the girls that belong to my church now, where I belong, they worked at the packinghouse. You know, almost any of these Baptist churches you go to, you're going to see somebody there you know, somebody you work with, or somebody you knew from a job. You always run into somebody that you know.

Most of the womens worked there were active in church and still is. When the packinghouse closed, and they was active in that, and they was active in the church, I guess they just kept being active, they wanted to be doing something, contributing something, so they kept going to church, since they didn't have no union or anything. They was active in the union because it was participating to their job, and then when the union went out, they didn't have no job for the union, then they was active in the church because that was their faith.

William Raspberry

Black economic advancement during and after World War II altered race relations in Kansas City and encouraged challenges to established patterns of racial discrimination. William Raspberry was a keen observer of, and participant in, this local civil rights movement. His daughter, of the same college generation as the protesters who sat in at lunch counters, was an active organizer of these protests. The UPWA was involved as well.

There were stores here you could buy stuff but you couldn't try it on, especially for women, and men, wouldn't let you buy a hat and try it on, you couldn't buy a suit and try it on. You could take it home, and they could find some reason for not wanting to take it back, so you'd have to pay for it whether you like it or not.

Then, during the war, they let them come in a lot of stores where they hadn't been welcome, women, because these women could get the jobs in the defense plants, and a lot of other industries opened up to them. They had a tale that said these women would go in these stores, worked for a couple of months, got all this money piled up, and then just bring it all and put it on the counter and say, "Sell me something for this money." Those stores who accepted money, their profit went up, and those who didn't said, well, look, the only thing that goes in the cash register is green, and we're missing out on that. So, they started too. This system was so greedy, boy, when money comes, if its available, don't everybody break down anything to get it.

Stores broke down, but it was in the '50's when the restaurants broke down because they started picketing. They started picketing department stores to go to the restaurants in the department stores. The first thing they did was to picket because we spend money here but we can't eat here. You've got to stand up and eat, we want to sit down and eat. I remember well, because my daughter was out of school that year. During a holiday that year, they said, don't shop here. Some people went in, but you'd be surprised at the number who didn't go in, and they felt it that year. Enough respected it for them to respect their wishes, and to grant concessions. That went on for months, right after Macy's came to town, I think that was the first one agreed to let blacks in.

There were several places where they would pick up people and take them downtown to different shifts on the picket. They had cars transporting them. My daughter was in the car pool, she was trying to help do the transporting to get them down there. It got to be fun, to be out there, and you see other blacks out there, it was really a fun thing to do.

See, the Brown case, *Brown versus Topeka, Kansas,* gave us more impetus to go ahead and push forward. Because if we're going to go to school together, we're going to be able to participate in all the other activities of a community. The black churches, as a rule, was the center of all the activities because they had to have some place to congregate. And, the black minister had certain influence on his congregation, so he could suggest that you do certain things. It's good that the churches was in it, because there were some militant people and the church recommended that we be decent about it, but be forceful. Not only ministers, but lawyers and teachers, everybody got involved. As a matter of fact, there was as many teachers on the picket line as there was anybody else. Urban League and the YMCA and the ministers, the NAACP, they were all involved.

The union got involved, the union got involved in everything. The union did some picketing. As a matter of fact, every time we'd have a meeting in any town, we'd picket against discrimination while we were there. We, the United Packinghouse Workers, broke down discrimination in the hotels in Kansas. One of the first hotels that admitted us was the Lima Hotel in Salinas, Kansas. And, of course, we voted to send a delegation down to thank Mr. Lima for opening up and to congratulate him for being courageous enough to do it. There were a lot of unions and, well, naturally, if all of them could stay in the same hotel, they would vote to go to that town, and they had more conventions there, and after they got more conventions in these different towns because they were integrated, it was to their advantage, financially. That's what you're in business for, to make a dollar.

The labor movement, we were sort of like an advisory to the [civil rights] movement, and we supplied the money. And we did marches, the labor movement, we would get into town and we would go and have our meetings, we would march, one day, against whatever it was the people in that community wanted us for. We were supposed to have membership in the NAACP and also membership in the Urban League. We worked in the confines of the organizations, whatever they were doing, we supported it.

81

Nevada Isom

Nevada Isom worked in the hog offal department of the Armour plant with Virginia Houston. She was a steward and member of the local union's bargaining committee and was active in community civil rights protests in the 1950s.

The whole group was involved, the bargaining committee and the executive board and all, to try to break down discrimination. We had these five- and ten-cent stores down there, I was involved in that. Farm Restaurant, on Main Street I believe, didn't hire black people as waitresses, and we weren't allowed to go in there and eat either, so I helped, I was in on that. The union rank-and-file members and stewards volunteered, they were there, and would want to participate.

William Raspberry

Raspberry considered one of his most important activities to be the pressure he exerted, along with another UPWA leader, on the United Auto Workers (UAW) to integrate the Kansas City automobile plants.

Henry McGraw (he was from Wilson) and I worked real close together. We was together on issues at the meetings because we would get together and talk; he lived about a block from me. Henry and I were obliged to attend at the Greater Kansas City Industrial Union Council at that time. Henry was more active than I. We fought, and we spoke up.

I think that Henry and I did as much to get blacks on the assembly line in the automobile industry as anybody. The UAW's policy on discrimination was one of the best, but the UAW's membership didn't go along with the policy. Blacks didn't participate, because they had that little clique. They were custodians, they was never laid off, and they worked and they had their own little kingdom there, and so they were happy. I used to tell them, "Well, what about all the people who are coming along, your kids, what are they going to do? You want them being a custodian?" We just drove CIO policy, and we said, if they can do it in the packinghouses they can do it in the other industries as well. We had some problems, yes, but we were still integrated.

We had a meeting there on Armstrong Avenue and Emil Mazey [UAW secretary-treasurer] came down and said we're going to integrate the assembly line and you guys go back in the plant and prepare your membership for it. They said well, they ain't going to accept it. He said, well they will. The day they integrated them, put the first black guy on, the management was objecting to it 'cause they knew they wouldn't get no production. Some of the guys walked off. He said, "Let 'em go. Hire somebody else in his place."

Raspberry's closing thoughts on unionism combined his awareness of race and class with an affirmation of the value of upward mobility in American society.

It gave me dignity. I felt like a human being, I felt like a person. Until I was in the union, I would have had to scratch and scratch and scratch. My daughter might have had to get a scholarship to go to college. As it was I was able to pay her way in. And I was able to give her enough money, and give her enough things, that she felt competent as anybody. I think there was either eight or twelve in that group my daughter went around with, and I was the only nonprofessional. But my daughter was accepted.

4

"I'VE BEEN AHEAD OF MY TIME"
Rowena Moore and Black Women's Activism in Omaha

Many of the UPWA's black leaders received their schooling in activism long before they entered the doors of a packinghouse or signed their first union card. In their own distinct ways, the black church, the Garvey movement, and the NAACP functioned as matrices of civil rights activism. Each institution battled for freedom and equality, produced an activist-oriented cadre, and helped shape the structure of black protest. Equally important was the black women's club movement that flourished in the early twentieth century. Decentralized and diffuse—and hence elusive for the historian—these clubs collectively formed one of the most enduring protest organizations in African American history.[1]

This chapter explores the singular career of Rowena Moore, a black woman from Omaha, Nebraska, who first became involved in protest activity through her association with two experienced club women. Moore's path crossed that of the UPWA for a fruitful but tension-fraught seventeen-year period. But long before her encounter with unionism, Moore had developed an unusual degree of confidence and consciousness of purpose. Her association with a number of small, sometimes informal club organizations endowed her with a sense of power and agency that allowed her to utilize her local union as a vehicle for protest and social change.

Born in rural Oklahoma in 1910, Moore moved with her family to Tulsa and then, in 1924, to Omaha. Her father joined hundreds of other black men for whom the city's stockyards and packinghouses represented a step up from farm work or common labor. Although her formative experiences took place in civic and social organizations, as a teenager Moore worked briefly at the local Cudahy plant. There, she received her first direct exposure to unionism. It was a time when the CIO was in its "heroic" phase, and the

Rowena Moore, 1986. *Photo by Rick Halpern.*

newly formed PWOC seemed to herald a new day for packinghouse workers. Moore remembered:

> The union was just getting organized good, and one of the things that
> impressed me, when Roosevelt was president—and I heard this with my
> ears—he said that if he was a working man, the first thing he would do
> would be to join a union. I heard that. And then, when the union people
> began to try to really organize and they were having trouble, it always kind
> of stayed with me that it was the right thing to do, to belong to a union.

An early marriage and the birth of a son, though, nudged Moore's trajectory
away from the industrial arena and back toward the world of women's clubs.

Leaving Cudahy, Moore came under the tutelage of Mrs. Bush and Mrs.
Wright, the two most important influences on her early development. In
addition to involving Moore in the local branch of the NAACP, children's
work, and several civic clubs, the older women opened up cultural vistas to
their protégé. The Garvey movement, the politics of W. E. B. Du Bois, black
folksong, and the poetry of Langston Hughes were topics of discussion in
the rooms above Mrs. Wright's tavern—a sort of African American Midwestern salon.

Moore's return to the packinghouse and union-centered activism during
the Second World War owed much to Mrs. Bush and Mrs. Wright. Follow-

ing the progress made by A. Philip Randolph's March on Washington Movement, the two older women turned their attention to securing employment for black women in Omaha's defense-related industries. The stockyards, which housed major plants of each of the Big Four packers, figured prominently in their plans. A well-organized strategy, worked out in tandem with packinghouse unionists, produced employment openings. Moore coordinated these efforts and, in late 1942, became one of the first black women to be hired at Armour and Company.

A seasoned organizer and an activist by temperament, Moore quickly became active in her union, UPWA Local 8. Coworkers elected her steward, she served as recording secretary, and she chaired the local's Human Relations Committee. During the UPWA's 1948 strike, she directed the local's entertainment committee. In the 1950s, she began to play an active role in the union's regional and national gatherings, speaking out forcefully on women's issues and linking them with the UPWA's commitment to anti-discrimination. She kept up her participation in the NAACP during this period and in fact solidified ties between the local branch and Omaha's packinghouse locals.

Yet these activities did not meet with universal approval. While their numbers were significant, black workers did not form the kind of critical mass in Omaha's packing plants that they did in Chicago and Kansas City. This meant that white unionists did not face the sort of rank-and-file pressure for aggressive, proactive implementation of the UPWA's anti-discrimination program that produced insurgency elsewhere. Omaha remained noticeably cool toward the sorts of civil rights campaigns that were a key feature of black unionism in the other packing centers. Indeed, Moore's very independence and grounding in organizations beyond the realm of the stockyards rendered her somewhat suspect in the eyes of local union officialdom. Her outspoken militancy and tireless action around women's issues further exacerbated this tension. Constant conflict, rather than mutual respect and cooperation, characterized Moore's relationship with the men who ran Local 8.

This history of friction and strain is indicative of larger tensions. The rise of industrial unionism in the meatpacking industry represented a genuine advance for black workers—both men and women. The grievance and seniority provisions of the contract allowed activists to eliminate many discriminatory practices and helped generate a rights consciousness that spurred a further round of struggle beyond the confines of the workplace. But during the organizing period and through the war years, women's concerns and grievances were articulated in the gender-neutral language of trade unionism in which men were assumed to be the typical union members. Moreover, the special needs of black women tended to be doubly masked: expressed in the first instance as unionists and then collapsed into—submerged really—within the struggle for racial equality. Rowena Moore's style of activism, which foregrounded her identity as a black woman, stretched the boundaries of the UPWA's brand of social unionism.

Moore was not alone. In the late 1940s and then increasingly in the 1950s, female packinghouse workers organized independently as women to prod a reluctant union bureaucracy to respond to their needs. Within an organization dominated by men, they fought for equal pay, challenged the sexual division of labor that prevailed in the plants, and struggled to reform a seniority system flawed by gender-based inequities. This feminist project was complicated by race. Rowena Moore's experience reveals the considerable gulf dividing black and white women in meatpacking. Given her relative isolation in Omaha, more often than not she was a lone voice. But her career also points to the ways in which she was able to transcend these obstacles and effect meaningful change.

Rowena Moore

We didn't come here 'til 24. We didn't come directly from the country; we came from Tulsa, Oklahoma. It was kinda nice to be in Omaha. We lived in south Omaha, and it was something a little bit different because we did have more white people in our area where we lived. In fact, we lived in a house that was owned by a white. Some black people owned their own homes, and it seemed to be a pretty stable neighborhood. The house we lived in in those days had a pump out in the yard, and everybody used the same outdoor toilets. The school was integrated—I hadn't been accustomed to that. As far as the children that we were in school with, they were nice; I had no problems at all with them. It was kind of nice being able to have them and to have a white teacher, 'cause we didn't have white teachers. It was kind of just something a little different.

My father, he worked at the packinghouse, and in a way we fared fairly well. My father bought a brand new convertible back in 1927, and he always had some car. He taught me how to drive at an early age. And I worked on cars, my father being a mechanic. People would stand back and ask my dad, "Does she know what she's doing?" And he said, "Oh, yeah, she knows what she's doing." I could listen to the car and tell what was wrong with it. And I would rather be out there working on somebody's car with my daddy, getting grease under my fingernails, than to be in the house washing dishes with my mother.

I've always down through my life been active in social and mostly civic things. I started early. Mrs. Loretta Bush and Mrs. Wright—Bear Cat Wright was a prizefighter—were active in civic and social things. Mrs. Bush took me to the first NAACP meeting in 1935, and in fact, I served as a secretary. At that time they only had about seventy-five members in the NAACP. That night they were talking about getting more people involved in it, and it met right down the street here in the church.

They were interested in people registering so they could vote. In fact, I went out when I was only fifteen years old to encourage them to go and register. We went from door-to-door. I was interested organizing the children, who did embroidering, crocheting, and anything like that, and I guess I just kind of stood out. I'm not bragging on it or anything, but this man came to me and told me, "We're going to be doing some visitation in the neighborhood and would you like to work with us," and naturally I enjoyed it. I also worked in the headquarters down on what was Q Street in South Omaha. Then, as time moved on, there were different stores that had inferior products that sold to neighborhoods where black people lived, and those things were worked on. And black people weren't served in restaurants and different other things. And then I guess it was about the fifties when Peony Park in Omaha was finally integrated. Those are the kind of things that happened.

Mrs. Wright had a tavern in South Omaha, and Mrs. Bush was active in a black civic organization, the Workmen's Club. They had their own building because Mrs. Bush had donated the building for them to use—a two-story building—and they had the beer tavern downstairs and then the club meetings upstairs, and Mrs. Bush lived in part of the building. She encouraged me to become a member of the Workmen's Club, which I did. And I was the secretary of it, too. They sold dinners and different things like that.

I lived in the project, and would come and go to my apartment, which was just across the street, and I'd stay a while and I'd come back. I'd come through the beer tavern, and I'd go back to Mrs Bush's apartment; I'd sit there and she'd talk to me. They had pictures of Marcus Garvey and showed them to me, and we talked about him. I was impressed about Garvey because he was a leader. I will always remember the first time I heard of Langston Hughes. She was telling me about Langston Hughes—that tells you the kind of person that she was. And you know the poem about life for me ain't been no crystal stair? "I had boards torn up, and splinters too, but all the time, honey, I's a-climbing. Turning corners, reaching, landing, sometimes traveling in the dark where there ain't been no light. But I's still a-climbing." And that poem has stayed with me, because that's the way life has been with me. I've done things, worked on things, I didn't have any guidance, any direction, nobody to tell me how to go and do it, you know. But I'm still climbing, still struggling, and getting splinters in my feet. I was bare, no shoes, you know. That poem always stuck with me.

We had another little club that was going under the Workmen's Club as the Defense Women's Club. That's what we called ourselves, and of course we were interested in the children. We sold ten-cent war bonds. And we'd encourage the children to bring some money and we'd sell them the stamps—they'd put it in their little books and start savings accounts. I thought we were really doing something; I hope it helped. [laughs] We formed a little group back during those early days. We called it "The Commandoes." And

Mrs. Bush and I would do the little things, little ice-cream socials, and raise a little money. And we bought some yards of cloth, in fact I still have a piece or two of it. And we made these little caps that soldiers wore. We made all of those kids one of those little caps out of that material. They were so proud of it! The kids would get out and they would march all around the blocks in the neighborhood. And me having a son, it really made it interesting because I believe that parents have to help their children to have friends. And if you let your neighbor's child go wrong, and your child is an associate of his, then your child will go wrong too. So you have to help your neighbors with their children in order to help your own son.

As a young person I always wanted to meet people who were interesting. I helped sponsor bringing W. E. B. Du Bois to Omaha. And I helped bring Marian Anderson, who sang down at the city auditorium. I was a young lady, but my son was about twelve years old then, and I remember, I think it was about five dollars. I paid for him to go along with me because I wanted him to have the opportunity to meet these prominent people. And I often think about the things that I tried to do to try to help further his education.

The Omaha packinghouses employed significant numbers of African Americans throughout the 1920s and 1930s. During the Second World War, the packers hired hundreds of additional black men to meet their burgeoning labor demands. Job opportunities for black women, however, remained more limited. In 1942, at the urging of Mrs. Bush and Mrs. Wright, Rowena Moore spearheaded a campaign to open up employment at the Armour plant for black women.

I was a young mother, I was twenty years old. I guess those women just got tired of me, always hanging round them instead of being out with other young women. I was always there with these old women. I was worrying them to death! One day they said, "We're going to try to help find some way you can get some jobs for these girls." And this was back in 1942, after the war started, and they came up with the idea that we should see if we can't get into the Armour plant. So they suggested I come out north—because this is where most of the black people lived—and they sent me out to recruit these women. They made arrangements for us to use a vacant building across from the plant. We'd go to the packinghouse, and they said, "That's all for today." That meant they weren't hiring any more.

So we'd go and they would go on across the street with me afterward and talk about what we ought to do and how we needed to approach it. Mrs. Bush and Mrs. Wright were giving us some counseling about how to try to dress and how to conduct ourselves. So many people had made a mistake—when they came to the packinghouse they heard there it was bloody and nasty so they could come in dirty clothes. It was very important that they learned that they didn't have to be unclean. They needed to know you don't wear wool clothes, and it's damp in there so you couldn't wear sandals, you need to put on shoes. And then you might have to have boots but they could buy them after they get there.

Crucial to the success of Moore's efforts was the assistance provided by black leaders of Armour Local 8. Aware of the pressure brought to bear on President Roosevelt to prohibit discrimination in defense-related industries, these unionists made use of the recently established Fair Employment Practices Commission (FEPC) created by Roosevelt's Executive Order 8802. Working in tandem with Moore, Local 8 prompted federal intervention into the dispute, which resulted in a government directive ordering the company to hire African American women.

I knew the men at the packinghouse because some of them had been friends to my father. So I talked to them and invited some union leaders to come and meet with us. I didn't try to get a job when we first started. I went to the employment office and sat there and watched what was happening, then I'd meet with the union men and tell them how many whites they'd hired that day. And no blacks. And what time we got out. I talked to them about us putting up a picket line. They said, "Well, you can't put up a strike, Rowena, because if you do, we want to honor your picket line. So don't do that, give us some time and let us work on it and see what we can come up with." The union officials went out and started talking to [Armour management], and the superintendent told somebody that there would never be any black women in Armour as long as he was superintendent. And hell, they didn't hire any until we put this pressure on them.

The union men came to my house one day, and we were talking about it. They said "Rowena, if you all will wait, give us some time to write to Chicago and see what we can find out." So they did. They wrote, and they said that there was something on the books that had been on there for some time but the president had never used it, and it would take some time for them to get the right contact in Washington. They told me, "Rowena, you find some girls that are about between twenty and twenty-seven years old, weigh about 115 or maybe 125 pounds." I had a cousin who recently had come from California, and she was living with me. Her name was Bedella Moore. Bedella fitted into that category, and in the meantime John Henry [a black officer in Local 8 and chief steward at the time], he knew another young lady named Emma Curtis, and he recruited her. They were the first two. So he said to me, "Have them be there at six o'clock, such and such a morning." We did, and they were the first two to be hired. And it really made me feel good because we were getting started. We were getting started!

This man from Washington came. He was a black man, and his name was Postum. He gave Armour and Company five days to get some black women in there, and then in three days they hired these two girls. At first they hired for a short time. Those two were the only two. Then I think they were laid off for a few days, then were hired back. Then, after a while, they started hiring more. That's what they had to do because they already had the law laid out, Executive Order 8802. The union handled it. I didn't have to do anything except wait—and that was the longest wait. They talked about waiting two weeks! That's too long! We got real energetic about it—we wanted it now! We felt like we'd been waiting forever as it was.

I'm very pleased about the support the union gave and always said that I'll always have a special love for the union because they did support getting the black women in there.

There were white women who said that they would not work with blacks—they would walk out. And the union told them that if they walked out, they'd be on their own, that they would not support them. And nobody walked out. Those women were cool, very cool, but then the dressing room was about the only place they really come in contact with them because they don't have many women on the kill. So if the union had not supported us, we would not have been able to get people in there at that time.

After we got these black women into the plant, then we started working to try to get black women into the front office, and you have to be a genius if you're black and want to get in the front office. You have to be a genius! I went out and did this search and found this lady, she had taught school and was a court recorder. She was A-1! And she got this job up at Armour's front office. She told me that those men would stand over her and watch her work. And that was the days when you didn't have any blacks in the front office.

Despite the assistance provided by John Henry and other African American union leaders, not all the men in Local 8 supported the drive to open employment to black women. Deeply ingrained patriarchal attitudes led many unionists to downplay the importance of women's work. Significantly, Moore detected differences in the sentiments of white and black men.

In those days there were many men—and some of our officials—who didn't believe that women really needed to work. The white men were more outspoken about it. Nels Peterson [a prominent Local 8 leader], his wife didn't work. He said, "Women ought to be at home preparing their husband's supper so when he comes up he can have a hot meal." Nels said that. There were others that felt pretty much the same way, they probably didn't have to say it. The black men knew that their women need to work, but they were not vocal about standing up and saying that women need to work. They might have did it—but I don't recall it. They had an integrated board at that time—Harrison Brown and Cecil Holloway—these black men were right up there with them.

Later in 1942, Moore began working in the Armour plant herself, laboring in the predominantly female offal department adjacent to the hog kill. There, her activist temperament brought her to the attention of coworkers, who elected her depart-

ment steward. She soon began to play a more direct role in the local union, serving for a period as recording secretary and, for a longer time, as chair of the Human Relations Committee. She brought a singular style of activism to this job, and her efforts on behalf of women workers sometimes brought additional conflict with both workmates and the men who controlled the local union.

I finally went to work at the packinghouse. They made me a steward because I was active in the different problems that they had and because I was concerned about the treatment of people, not just black people but whoever it was. I worked on the hog kill—in the offal, the casing department—but if a problem come up, you could go where you wanted. I worked all over. If someone came to me with a problem, I would take it up. I had cases where the union would not support me, so I didn't discuss it with them. The men would come to me faster than the women. The women were very passive—I don't know what would have to happen before they complained! It was the men that usually had the problems. And you can't fight a case unless the people are willing to support it. You'll go out there and get blown away.

They would send girls to work with me—the foreman would say, "Rowena, teach her how to do this, show her how to do this." Sometimes they would send me foreigners and I would teach them. Some of the white women wouldn't, they didn't want to having nothing to do with foreigners. They would make remarks about me. They'd call me "D. P." [Displaced Person] because I'd get acquainted with them and get along fine—they'd be new, they hadn't been in the country but two or three days. I learned to talk to them with signs. I didn't have anything against those people. If I'd go to someplace, I'd want somebody to teach me how to do my job. So I just treated them the way I felt I'd want to be treated, and I just ignored all this yelling across the room making remarks about me. But they would sometimes have jobs that were overloaded, and they would need some help. They had guidelines saying that they were supposed to have two people doing it, but they would let them work all by themselves without trying to give them any relief. That was part of my trouble.

Another thing that I did that helped a lot of people: They had a guideline where you worked thirty days before you could become a member of the union. And on the twenty-eighth or twenty-ninth day, I knew they were going to lay them off. You was not going to be there on the thirtieth day. So I kept time on these girls that worked with me, and I would ask to be off on business—I couldn't afford it, but I was being off so that that person could have an opportunity to work and get her seniority. They wouldn't lay her off because they had to have certain number of people to do the job. I didn't just do this once; I did this many times to help them get their thirty days in.

The other thing I did was when I found out we didn't have to work more than nine hours, I went home every day at four-thirty. Even when we had only twenty minutes more to work, I still sacrificed so that I could let these other people know that they did not have to stay there and work ten or twelve hours just because they got a lot of hogs in. I'd always throw up my hand and say, "Hey, I'll see you tomorrow!" to let everybody know that I was going. I felt that somebody had to be an example, somebody had to prove to them that you don't have to work—and the couple of more dollars that I could have made could done me a lot of good, but I felt what I could do to help these other people to learn their rights would be more valuable.

There was a guideline that they had to furnish a place for women to rest or sit anytime it didn't interfere with their production. I was the first one to use that. They talked about me; they tried to say that I wanted to sit down because I had this problem with my feet. But that was not the problem at all—I was concerned because I had this book from the State of Nebraska saying that women's rights was this that and the other, and I was trying to implement this.

Shortly after I went into the plant, I was elected [recording] secretary for a number of years, and the only reason I didn't get reelected was because they nominated me and I declined. I told them that a woman could do something in that local beside being the secretary. I felt a woman should be eligible to do something else—then later I was elected chair of human relations. I didn't feel that just because you're a woman then that's the only thing that you can do. I believe that women have rights. A lot of times people think it was just since the 1970s that they've started working on issues for women: I've been ahead of my time.

Beginning in the late 1940s, the seniority provisions of the UPWA's master agreements emerged as a source of tension within the union. Separate male and female seniority lists meant that women with many years of service could be laid off in favor of men with less seniority. In the 1950s, when the packinghouse workforce began to shrink, the seniority issue became especially contentious. Moore was outspoken in her opposition to dual lists, arguing for a single system in front of the UPWA's 1952 convention. This stand further exacerbated tensions between her and other unionists.

Finally, I found out about the seniority list. I went to the convention that was held in Denver, Colorado. And they were talking about these seniority lists. I went to the microphone and I spoke about women should be on the one seniority list; they should avoid that separate list. I knew that we paid the same amount of [dues] money that the men paid. We put in the same hours that they worked. And they usually put the women and the black people on the hardest or the worst jobs—something nobody else want. Of course, if you're at the top of the seniority list, you can have your choice and refuse this, and that means that that black person or that woman has to take whatever they can get because they want to work. And I felt that as long as

94

these were the facts in the case, that we deserved the same consideration that anybody else would get. So why have us on one seniority list when, they cut the gang, out goes these people and here comes this man who's come on the job a month ago and they're laying me off! And I've been paying my union dues and supporting the union! I felt that we deserved that same consideration regardless of what you are—a woman or man, black or white, or whatever. I felt it was worth fighting for.

Now, I was absolutely booed on that floor! I couldn't help but cry because it hurt me. When I came back to my plant and told them I had said this, they kind of pooh-poohed it off. Men don't come back from the convention and tell you things of importance—they come back and tell you that they played the Star Spangled Banner, and some minister prayed, and the mayor came and gave the welcome, and we broke up into committees. And that's just about all they tell you. And here I am coming up with this other stuff and it's, "Don't pay no attention to her."

The men fought me as hard as they could. Those men had it made. It was certain men that went to the convention, even though you would have an election. I had to work hard at going to conventions. It got to the point where we had a rule where the union had to have women in the delegations. So if a woman was elected, I automatically got a chance to go, but I had to work hard at it. See I covered both spots—you had to have women and you had to have minorities. But if it weren't for that guideline, I wouldn't have gotten to go.

The union was not very happy with some of the things the people did. For example, another thing that I did was I wrote a letter to the Hinky Dinky store up here on 30th and Park, talking to them from my Human Relations Committee about hiring a black person in an administrative position. And he returned a letter to me sometime later saying that we have hired our first black manager. I still have that letter, and I was very pleased about that.

Now see, the union didn't do a lot of these things. I'm the one that did them. And it wasn't something that the union suggested that I do. It was just that I was concerned—not to say that I'm all that brighter than everybody else, but I've always from my early years liked organizational work, and every opportunity I had I was involved in something that I thought might be of some benefit. I was associated with these older women, which made it good because it fitted right in.

I've had some terrible hurts, terrible hurts, and most of that came from the leadership of the union. I'm thankful that I lived through it, because if I had been a weak person, things would have been altogether different—they would have drove me out of the packinghouse.

Moore remained active in the Omaha NAACP while working at Armour. In the early 1950s, she recruited large numbers of packinghouse workers into the Association, transforming its class character and outlook. This change alarmed the black professionals and middle-class white liberals who previously had run the organization. Moore recalled that whites outnumbered African Americans on the NAACP Board before the 1950s and discussed their worried response to the influx of black packinghouse workers.

I don't think there were many blacks in it back in those days; there were white people. They hired a director, someone who was black, but the board and everybody was professional and salaried kind of people. They didn't know what was going on. Those people looked down on packinghouse people. I attended meetings, and when I did, people said, "Miss Moore, what do you do?" I'd say "Oh, I work in the packinghouse." "Oh, I didn't think packinghouse people was interested in anything like this!" People think "packinghouse people," and they didn't realize that some of our best lawyers have worked in the packinghouse, some of our teachers left the packinghouse and went to teach in school. And they were glad to get those packinghouse jobs. No, I don't think they knew what was going on.

The NAACP was very small back in the forties. I took in more members to the NAACP—I took 150 people in at the packinghouse about 1955. The union supported me; I talked to the management, and they let me set up a table in the plant. And I took in more than the whole NAACP together— they only had a few members. [NAACP President] Mark McVoy had said, "Listen, let's don't let them packinghouse people get control of this NAACP. We has to vote 'em down; we can't let these packinghouse people get in control of things." I guess he was afraid that he'd lose his base. You know, he could talk and fiddle around, and find out everything and get his little group together. We used to say he'd carry the NAACP around in his hip pocket.

The NAACP had said that they would pay $150 to the person who brings in the most memberships. So I'm the one that brought in the most memberships. And Mark McVoy got up and made a motion that he knew that the packinghouse people was going to help me, and that they should cut my award. I didn't argue with them; they cut it down. Instead of $150 they gave me $125. That happened. But that's the way things go.

The Omaha packinghouse locals, especially Armour Local 8, stood at the forefront of the anti-communist opposition within the UPWA. Moore's outspokenness, visibility, and independent actions made her a target for white conservatives within her local. Never affiliated with the organized Left, she explained that she was always open to pragmatic alliances.

I worked with everybody. One of the things that I was always concerned about was the nondiscriminatory attitude of people, and that always touched me. When you get on discrimination and trying to break down discrimination, and trying to get people equal rights, you'd get my ear. You could always attract my interest if you were working in something like that. I wanted to hear it. I don't have to be a part of it exactly, but I needed to know about it.

I've been called everything, but it really didn't bother me, because I felt just like we feel about religion, and with me being black and you being an Italian and him being a Jew or whatever it is, I felt that this was only another kind of racial thing, or way that people had about avoiding whatever it is that they might need to be participating in or doing.

When we'd go to a convention out of town, we were watched. Blacks were watched. Nels Peterson, Red Lockhart, and the white people in Local 8 didn't want black people to have a meeting. They wanted us to have all open meetings; they didn't want no private kind of meeting. They watched you like you was a criminal. But I just have always felt that I didn't need to let any of those kind of things deter me from doing what I felt I had to do.

Recurrent medical problems forced Rowena Moore to leave meatpacking in 1959. A modest pension coupled with disability payments allowed her to devote most of her time to politics and women's issues. She was active in the founding of the

Rowena Moore and Dwinton Davidson from the Armour local in St. Joseph, Missouri, at the UPWA's 1957 anti-discrimination conference. *Used with permission of the State Historical Society of Wisconsin [WHi (X3) 50377].*

Coalition of Labor Union Women (CLUW), played a role in the National Organization for Women (NOW), and worked tirelessly to inject a black female presence into her local Democratic Party organization. For more than 20 years, her most cherished project has been the creation of a memorial honoring Malcolm X, who was born in Omaha just a short distance from Moore's home.

I left the plant on disability—my feet were giving me trouble, and I came out to have surgery and was never able to go back. In the first few years I was out of the plant, I handled cases on the telephone. Workers having problems on the job with different things would call me and I'd advise them.

Back in the late sixties my sister read a biography of Malcolm [X] and found that his daddy's address was 3448 Painton Street and she called me. I wanted to make this memorial. My family is donating this ground. We have six lots out there that is 124 feet deep and 50 feet wide and the street is in between. And when we get all of that in, and there's an area out there of forty blocks. And we are hoping to use all of that area for the development for Malcolm X. We don't own it, we only own that six blocks. But my plans and my thought is that this is important enough that in Omaha, Nebraska, this would help tourism, and it would give black people wherever they lived some place to be proud of. I'm hoping that before this year's gone we'll have a park, covering and including the area of 3448 Painton where he was born.

I felt that Malcolm was a person that was trying to get the attention of black people to help us feel that we are important, too. And that we have to treat ourselves with respect. And I think that he got the attention of a lot of young people, and I feel that that's something worth remembering. The other thing is I felt that he got their attention enough to realize we have something to be proud of, too. And I feel that Malcolm is the person that aroused people's attention. He aroused their attention in the very beginning by talking about white people.

I'm a person who was here when [U.S. Senator Theodore] Bilbo was running and campaigned. I heard Bilbo on the radio talking about "my niggers," they'd better not do this and they gonna do that. "My niggers." And I felt that if Bilbo can talk like that and get elected, I can't hold Malcolm responsible for what he said. And he did get attention. A good politician gets your attention any way he can get it. He might tell you something that is not exactly what he'd want to be saying. But if he wanted to get elected, he'd got to get your attention. So I look at it from a political angle. But if we can forgive Bilbo, reelect him to his national position, why can't you forgive a black person?

I don't have any support for separatism. I can wholeheartedly support Malcolm X because in his last days he changed from being a separatist. He realized that you did not have to be black to be a good person; he was willing to accept other people. I give him credit for making advancements. As he learned, he made changes in his life. Malcolm changed as he moved, and he changed several times in life. I congratulate him for it because I felt that each of those changes was a step forward and a step for betterment. And I feel that as far down the rung as Malcolm was, he came up to help other people. People could take example of it. They don't have to do the bad things but take the good of whatever he did or said, and put that to good use. I think that's what's important in life. I think we all get some ill advice from time to time, but you live over those things and you do not try to go and make the same kind of mistakes that someone else made. I'm not encouraging people to follow Malcolm's footsteps as such, to make the same mistakes. I think that he would not want us to do that. I think he would want us to better our condition. I think he would want us to do what we can do to help each other and be proud of ourselves.

Despite the opposition and occasional hostility she encountered from many of Local 8's leaders, Moore recognized that the union provided her with an institutional base for social change. For a 17-year period in her long career as an activist, the UPWA served as a vehicle through which she could mobilize other African American workers, gain a hearing for her views, and ally with other black organizations. She struck a philosophical note when reflecting on her stormy association with the labor movement.

If you're not satisfied with something, you don't just pack up your books and go home. You work with that group and try to change it or do something to improve it. And I don't think you have to agree with everything that the packinghouse people do to work with the packinghouse union. I think it's like a marriage—you don't agree with everything that your wife or husband do, but you don't get mad an kill 'em or walk off. You stay there and you work together the best you can. So that's one reason I've worked with these organizations, because I find that there's something in them that's for the betterment of the people that I am close to and that I love. I don't see any other way to do these things to help make this a better world.

5

"INSTEAD OF CRUMBS WE WANTED US A SLICE OF THE PIE"
The Struggle for Black Equality in Fort Worth

As in northern cities, the packinghouse industry in Fort Worth, Texas, represented a major source of employment for blacks. The largest southern outpost of the industry, Fort Worth contained major plants operated by Armour and Swift and a sprawling stockyards complex. At its peak in the mid-1940s, nearly three thousand workers labored in Fort Worth's packinghouses, fertilizer plants, glue works, and cattle pens. Approximately a third of the workers were African Americans, many of whom had migrated to central Texas from other parts of the South. Another one-half of the workers were native-born whites, most of whose families had lived in the Dallas–Fort Worth area for several generations. Several hundred Spanish speakers, hailing from lower Texas and the Southwest, completed the packinghouse workforce.[1]

Despite its size and importance as a packing center, the organization of Fort Worth proved an elusive goal. Soon after the opening of the stockyards, a 1904 union campaign directed by the AFL's Amalgamated Meat Cutters ended in dismal failure. In 1921 and 1922, another drive faltered when the packing companies effectively manipulated antagonisms among the deeply divided workforce. The major cleavage ran along racial lines, with most black workers remaining aloof from what they perceived to be the "white man's union." Violence repeatedly flared as scores of black strikebreakers crossed the Amalgamated's picket lines and hundreds more passed directly into the stockyards aboard special trains. The local Ku Klux Klan took part in the intimidation of African Americans seeking to take advantage of the labor conflict to secure employment. In the strike's final days, a mob of whites removed an injured black worker from a local hospital and lynched him near the stockyards. Long after Fort Worth's packinghouse workers returned to their jobs, lingering animosities and mutual suspicions checked attempts to rekindle unionism.

Only in the late 1930s, when the PWOC began its push into the South, did Fort Worth's black, white, and Mexican-American workers take their first steps toward interracial accommodation and even solidarity. Packinghouse unionism in the city was always limited; it never extended to the Swift plant, where paternalistic company policies led workers to support the National Brotherhood of Packinghouse Workers, and the stock handlers local, although part of the UPWA, remained a white job preserve until its disaffiliation from the International union in the mid-1950s. The UPWA presence in Fort Worth revolved around the local union at Armour and, because of demographics and its location in the Jim Crow South, followed a trajectory significantly different than the one followed in the Midwestern packing centers.

The material benefits unionism provided to the rank and file provided the foundation for the coalition of racial groups that made up the Fort Worth Armour union. The CIO's ability to deliver wage increases, benefits, and a degree of control over the pace and intensity of work was the glue that held different sections of the workforce together in a fragile alliance.

However, in the late 1940s and early 1950s, the implementation of a civil rights program within the union shattered the racial equilibrium prevailing in Fort Worth and starkly revealed the boundaries and limitations of the interracial movement there. Subject to severe stress and strain, the coalition ruptured, with white workers withdrawing from active participation. In the highly charged southern atmosphere of the 1950s, black and Mexican-American workers eagerly embraced the civil rights program of the International union, using it as a lever with which to redress long-standing racial grievances, even though such advances were purchased at the cost of diminished white support.

The Fort Worth experience of black packinghouse workers reveals how southern racial dynamics differed from those prevailing in the Midwestern packing centers. It also shows that labor-based civil rights activism still could proceed in the face of intense opposition.

Frank Wallace

Frank Wallace was a founder of Local 54 in the Fort Worth Armour plant. Born in 1921, he followed his father, a laborer at Swift, into the city's packinghouses. At the age of 18, Wallace began working on Armour's loading dock, where his hourly wage of 48 cents an hour compared favorably with that paid black men in other southern industries. Along with George Thomas, also a member of the loading dock gang, Wallace formed part of the core of black unionists in the plant. After the union won a representation election in early 1943, Wallace served as a depart-mental steward. Later, workers elected him chief plant steward and local vice pres-ident. The International union hired Wallace as a field representative in 1954, and after the 1968 merger, he continued to work for the Amalgamated Meat Cutters. He served as a field representative for the United Food and Commercial Workers following the establishment of that organization in 1979. He retired in 1984.

When I went there, it hadn't been quite a year since I finished high school. It was a job that paid relatively more than some of the little menial jobs like a filling station, or cleaning some drugstore or some office building. In this area, the packing plant jobs and the railroad was about the best you could find.

Inside the plant, the hardest and the dirtiest jobs were always given to the blacks and other minorities, especially the kill floor and the hide cellar, the tank house, and the jobs that were on the loading dock, where there was heavy work. I would say that anywhere from 75 to 85 percent of the employ-ees in those departments were either black or Mexican-Americans. There were not any blacks or minorities on any of the checking jobs or the scaling jobs; the only jobs we had were luggers for lugging the steers and the hogs. There were other departments of the plant, like sliced bacon, which was con-sidered a clean area, where there were no blacks at all, no minorities whatso-ever in that department. There were also no blacks in the mechanical depart-ments; we had a small electrical department, and there was no blacks in there either. So, blacks and minorities had all the dirty and heavy jobs. That's the way they had the whole setup in the plant.

I was bitter against the treatment that I was getting from the top boss on that loading dock. I was a young fellow who did need that job real bad, but I certainly didn't appreciate the way I was having to be talked to every day. I think his every second word was a curse word, and when he would give you orders he had to use some of his foul language, which was very upsetting to most of us, especially those that were young in age.

But it was a job, so you swallowed your pride, and you stayed there. And I would have done anything—if it had been a little green man from some other planet with a union card, I would have signed it and helped him try to get a union in, especially when they told me that some of that stuff I was tak-ing down there I wouldn't have to take if we were able to get the union in. At the same time I didn't have fear of any individual, and I didn't go along with the things that the old-time blacks were going for at that time. I couldn't cope with that kind of situation, and that made me real interested in becom-ing involved in the union.

The loading dock, along with the beef, hog, and sheep killing departments, quickly emerged as a center of union strength, partly because of the structure of the work process in meatpacking. The heavy concentration of black and Mexican-American workers was another important factor behind the militancy of these departments.

Regardless of what happened in the other departments, that product had to be shipped out of the loading dock, and if it got blocked there, well there was no use killing or processing the meat. On the killing floors, there's always pressure because the need is so great for the product to get out. Any of the areas where they've got to depend on product getting out, there's always pressure applied by the bosses. So naturally it's one of the reasons for those workers becoming aggressive. They want some kind of relief for the pressure, from the foot that's on their head, and they're willing to take a chance of doing something about it.

Basically the ones who would take the chances and be ready to organize were the blacks and the minorities. Whites would take the backseat. Later, if things were rolling on pretty smooth with the bosses, then they might accept the organization.

Whites were skeptical; they had a greater fear of their bosses than blacks or minorities. They might have seen the need for changes, but they were not the ones who wanted to step out in front and begin a program, or begin an organizing drive that's going to help the situation. If you pushed them enough, they might get behind you if you stepped out in front, but normally they would not step out. I found that after I started working full-time for the unions, it was the same all over, regardless of where I was.

Armour vigorously resisted the union campaign. In addition to employing spies, discharging activists, and sponsoring a company union, management deliberately tried to foster racial antagonism.

It was an everyday thing with them. They would constantly say to the whites that the union will force us to put blacks or some of these Mexicans on your jobs, that they might take them away from you. Prior to organization, there were differences in the wages paid for the same job, or jobs that were similar. And the company would tell them that if the union came in they would have to start paying blacks and Mexicans the same rate. So they played not only the race thing, one against the other, but also the wage thing as well.

Mary Salinas

Mary Salinas, a Mexican-American, was born in Rosebud, Texas, in 1922 and grew up in Waco. Her father was a painter and an active unionist who was forced to flee Waco in the wake of Ku Klux Klan terror there. The Salinas family settled in Dallas, and in 1942 Mary began working at Armour in the beef cut department. She was one of the few women active in the founding of the local, playing an important role recruiting women and other Spanish speaking workers. She served as a steward in the 1940s and early 1950s. Coworkers elected her president of the local in 1954, a position she held until 1963 when Armour closed the Fort Worth plant. Retrained as a cosmetologist under a program established by the Armour Automation Committee, Salinas worked at this trade until 1965. She then returned to the meatpacking industry, working first at Standard Meat and more recently at Alston Beef. Both were nonunion firms.

Like many union founders, Mary Salinas stressed issues of human respect when discussing the reasons behind her decision to take part in the PWOC drive. She began her narrative by recalling the "terrible" working conditions inside the plant in the early 1940s.

There was no consideration of human beings, and the language they used wasn't limited just to men. My foreman, he has passed away now and I hope he's forgiven, but Mr. Davis would never call us by our names, and that's rough when you have to make a living for that price. To go through all of that, it's rough.

And the women had special problems, like the pregnancy issue. When they became pregnant, not only if they were a single person but if they were married, they would get fired. And then a lot of women had problems, too, losing their babies before delivery time [because they remained at work], and there too they would get fired because they stayed off the job. Even if they were in the hospital! I was in the hospital and they let me go. The company said that I didn't have no business being in the hospital!

We did as well as we did because of the black people, they really had the push. We had a strong union because of the black people. The departments where there were no Negroes were weak. Regardless of what you wanted to do, those departments would not support you on anything.

We didn't have very many departments that weren't strong, just sliced bacon where the majority of the people were women and they were white, and they were just there for the almighty dollar. They didn't care. They were young women, and the foreman sugarcoated them all the time. The foremen would use them in order to keep them weak.

Although the sliced bacon department remained a thorn in the union's side for many years, most white workers came to support the PWOC. Salinas was instrumental in recruiting previously aloof whites on the beef cut and elsewhere in the plant. The key to winning white support was emphasizing the material benefits afforded by union organization.

I knew that the only thing that would really get them enthused would be to mention money. And I used it. Most people you can say, well, we'll get hospitalization, we'll get leaves, we'll get more vacation, but they're really not interested at the moment with that. But when you mention that their salaries are going to go up, they start listening. And so I used that method. I would mention money and then I'd go on down to other benefits that I wanted for myself, and I was sure, as a worker, that they would want to get those things too. And that's how I got them to work with us.

In mid-1943, under pressure from the National War Labor Board and packing-house locals throughout the Armour chain, Fort Worth management capitulated and recognized the union after it registered a dramatic National Labor Relations Board election victory. No wage increase followed, but recognition and coverage by a strong contract were significant gains in themselves. Mary Salinas put it succinctly, stating that "to me, the recognition meant more than if they had given us a dollar an hour raise, because they recognized us as a group, as a union."

This new institutional footing did not lead to cordial industrial relations. The union continued to rely on job actions and other displays of power at the point of production to enforce the contract and to compel management to negotiate with departmental stewards over shop-floor conditions. Some job actions took place during the Second World War, despite the labor movement's formal agreement not to engage in strikes during wartime. Workers like Mary Salinas saw little contradiction between their actions and their support for the war effort. Rather, they believed that reciprocal obligations were involved and that the company was to blame.

It wasn't just a one-way street, you know. And if they able to violate their commitment, what would be wrong with us violating ours, too? And we did have quite a bit of stoppages, and in fact I would encourage them. I encouraged them because of the number of hours they were working the people with the number of employees. Some of the employees had to be doubling up into three jobs, and that was unreasonable. They wasn't going to work those people day and night and we wasn't going to do nothing about it.

These wartime stoppages tended to be well planned and orchestrated actions rather than spontaneous displays of workers' frustration.

Frank Wallace

There were times in some departments where we had disagreements with management on grievances, so we had some sit-downs. We backed up against the wall and refused to work until our grievances could be heard, and a lot of times settled before we would go back to work. At that time, I didn't consider it a violation of the [no-strike] pledge. They didn't last long enough to actually cause any major problems for the military, but they were necessary in order to correct unjust things that had been placed on the employees at that time. We had become quite strong in our belief in getting fair treatment.

I wasn't the only steward in that department; we had five or six. We tried to have one for every ten workers. Sometimes the job action would come from the local executive board and sometimes it would come from the chief steward, with the assistance of the department steward. Those kind of actions were more or less planned to the extent that we would sometimes have meetings prior to doing these things to make sure that they come off as they should. The real burning type of grievance were those where people were denied the rate on the particular jobs, the company refusing to pay them the correct rate. Also when promotions had been denied, we had some real hot meetings on those kind of things. Some of the other things that would be hot issues would be the overtime hours, where in some departments they would keep the people almost there nineteen to twenty hours a day almost, seven days a week at a time. So those were some of the hottest issues that we more or less got into. It wasn't easy. Those settlements had to result from sit-downs or standing up against the wall instead of working, in order to get the management's attention, to see that what they were doing wasn't right, wasn't justified.

Responding to wartime labor shortages, many women, most of them African Americans, joined the packinghouse workforce. The company's efforts to capitalize on cheap female labor generated grievances over equal pay for equal work.

During the war there were quite a few women hired in, and they continued to work there afterwards. A large percentage of them worked on jobs that had normally been done by men—jobs in the hide cellar, spreading hides, salting hides down, hauling hides from the kill floor areas, and washing down the killing floors. They weren't paid the same as men; they were paid less. That was one of the big fights that we had locally, and also in national negotiations, as to comparable rates.

Eddie Humphrey

The war also had a major impact on packinghouse unionists who left the plant for military service. For many black workers, the experience of fighting a segregated "war for democracy" changed the way in which they regarded their place in southern society.

Eddie Humphrey was part of a large cohort of black workers that entered the meatpacking industry during and immediately following World War II. Although he worked briefly in meatpacking before enlisting in the army, Humphrey had little contact with the union. His military service was a formative experience, one that oriented him toward activism. He emerged as an important leader of the Fort Worth union in the 1950s, serving as departmental and divisional steward and as a local officer.

I went abroad; I fought. I was an honorable-discharge veteran. I went overseas on a ship called the *U.S.S. Lejune,* and all of us black soldiers on that ship, we called it "in the belly of a whale" because we were down below the surface of the water. If we had been torpedoed, that would have been it. It was impossible to try to come up the stairs; we were down about two flights; that's where we had to sleep. Even though I love this country, I've always respected it, but I had learnt something also. Being in that type of a war, and what we were fighting for—to rid the country of Nazism and Communism—and when I came back I just couldn't see myself being segregated and discriminated against the way we were. And that's why I became so close with the union. We died, our blood had been shed for this country, and I felt that we should get a better deal out of it. Instead of crumbs, we wanted us a slice of the pie.

Invigorated by the renewed activism of veterans, blacks in the Fort Worth Armour local began to push forward demands for an end to racial discrimination in the plant. Using the seniority provisions of the contract, "We proceeded to ask for those jobs that in the past had been off-limits for us," recalled Frank Wallace. "I think that's about the time that we began to recognize that we had a little bit more muscle, a little bit more people power, let's say, than we had before."

L. C. Williams was another black army veteran who emerged as a leader in the Fort Worth Armour plant after the war. The son of sharecroppers in east Texas, Williams labored at a number of industrial jobs in the Port Arthur–Beaumont region before enlisting in the military in 1943. Upon his discharge at the war's end, he moved to Fort Worth and found employment at Armour. Working on the loading dock with Wallace and George Thomas, he typified the younger, more militant African American workers who wanted to use their union to end segregation and discriminatory treatment.

L. C. Williams

We wanted our voice recognized. We wanted our membership to be counted for something rather than just getting our dues, and we was constantly making noise about it. Pressure was put on the International union to negotiate a contract deal, remove all [Jim Crow] signs from the plant, eliminate dual [wage] rates among the blacks and the whites—if you was a splitter on the floor, you didn't get the same rate of pay that the skilled whites did. Even the Mexican people were affected by it, so we had some help on that thing.

Mexican-American workers' support for anti-discrimination initiatives was important because it helped shift the balance of power within the Fort Worth Armour local, but it was fraught with complications stemming from the peculiar-

ities of southern segregation. Frank Wallace pointed out that more Mexican-Americans found employment in meatpacking as a result of wartime labor shortages but that their loyalties were divided. "Some stood with the blacks, some with the whites. Because at that time in this area, Mexican people had been brainwashed to the extent that they considered themselves white. Some believed it and some did not, so it was divided." Mexican-Americans occupied an ambiguous domain in the structure of Jim Crow—allowed to drink out of "white" water fountains and stay at "white" hotels, but still treated as second-class citizens. In meatpacking and other industries, they often labored on jobs regarded as unsuited for white workers. After World War II, Mary Salinas began to assume a visible leadership role in the local, working to throw the weight of the Mexican-American membership behind a more aggressive civil rights program.

Mary Salinas

You know, I had quite a struggle. The different names that I was called! Well, I tried to ignore them, but I'm a human being, too. What names I was called because I was for the Negro people! I felt that if we could work together, we could eat together at the same table. You can socialize with them, you can eat with them, you can work with them, and I'm sure we're going to either hell or heaven with them. I still feel that way, and not only because I was in the union. I still feel it in the same way.

Black and Mexican-American activism in the postwar period clashed with the sensibilities of many white workers. The extent of these tensions first surfaced during the UPWA's 1948 strike. Frank Wallace recalled that as the strike began to crumble, one group of racist whites attempted to engineer a back-to-work movement in order to "be able to get rid of all the Niggers" and that the resulting friction began to erode solidarity between the races. "There seemed to be a lot of hostility building up, a lot of hatred over and above what had already been there. So this caused us not only a problem we had to deal with in regard to management, but also a problem in our own ranks." For their part, many black workers began to question the ability and commitment of the largely white local executive board.

L. C. Williams

We had some shabby leadership at that time. It was whites running it, a guy by the name of Moon Mullins, Collins, and Dorothy Bobo. I remember only two blacks who had any position, and they wasn't on the finance side or strategy; they were picket captains and stuff like that.

The 1948 strike was a turning point for the Fort Worth local. In the aftermath of the strike, black workers in Fort Worth used the anti-discrimination initiatives of the International union to press for changes in the Armour plant. However, District Director A. J. Pittman and his staff only gave lip service to civil rights and were reluctant to move forward with any concrete programs.

Mary Salinas

He [Pittman] didn't want us to go too fast—that's his words, "too fast"—because we kept putting pressure on him that we wanted those [Jim Crow] partitions removed [from the plant cafeteria]. He said that there would be a lot of dissension in the membership, that there would be lots of withdrawals and all that. We went on pushing for it and he didn't want to move; so we had to bring in the International.

C. B. McCafferty, a stock handler who, along with his father, was one of the staunchest supporters of egalitarian unionism, recognized Pittman's dilemma.

C. B. McCafferty

Pittman was in a bad position here. I don't knock him about his cautiousness. This was Texas and you didn't jack with it, you just tried to do small things. They might be desegregating the whole plant in Chicago, but down here they desegregated the cafeteria or the vending machines.

Because of their alliance with black activists in other UPWA plants and their participation in Armour "chain" negotiations, Fort Worth unionists were able to overcome Pittman's intransigence. In 1952, national negotiations with Armour resulted in an agreement mandating desegregation of all plant facilities. This victory was won "over the heads" of Director Pittman and his allies.

L. C. Williams

It was all done through negotiations, and fortunately our local committees were more powerful in that regard with the International's top negotiators than the directors were—I'm sure that if Pittman had anything to do with it, we never would have had it in the contract. We would always elect our committees from the plant locally, and then we would go to the national negotiations with Armour and Company as a group from various parts of the country.

An already racially tense situation exploded in Fort Worth within weeks. In November 1952, management removed signs designating "White Only" and "Colored" facilities and announced that the plant cafeteria would be desegregated the following month. The backlash was immediate: angry whites demanded that the union direct the company to replace the signs and leave the cafeteria partition in place. When local leaders balked, the protesters organized themselves into a "Local Rights" committee led by union officers Moon Mullins and Dave Collins. This group appealed directly to Armour; two days later the signs reappeared. Seething, black workers threatened a walkout. The crisis intensified as rumors spread to other southern plants and a regional disaffiliation movement began to form. "The heat was really there," Frank Wallace remembered, "racism was there like it had never been before." To force the company to implement the agreement, UPWA president Ralph Helstein telephoned Armour Vice President Frank Green and threatened to strike other Armour plants.

Ralph Helstein

"You and I got a date to go to Fort Worth. We've got a lot of trouble there." He [Frank Green] said, "I understand you got some troubles down there, but they're not my troubles." And I said, "Oh, Frank, you're wrong. You've got troubles, too. And you had better *make* them your troubles, or, if you prefer, I'm going to pick up this telephone and I'm going to call every Armour local in the United States and tell them you are reneging on your agreement about eliminating segregated dining rooms."

Helstein's ultimatum brought a quick response from Armour. The Fort Worth plant superintendent was ordered once again to remove the Jim Crow signs, and Armour's top management journeyed to Texas to meet with UPWA leaders and defuse the racist revolt. The meeting at the union hall was tense and now occupies a prominent place in the oral tradition of the area. "There were knives and guns all over the place. There was screaming and hollering. It was impossible to keep order," Helstein remembered.

L. C. Williams

Everybody held their ground. [UPWA Vice President Russell] Lasley did a beautiful job, saying, "This is part of the contract now. This is what we are going to live by, and the company is going to live with this contract too. They're going to enforce it because they agreed to it, just like we did." Finally Dean Hawkins came down—he was the vice president of Armour at that time—and that was really the end of it. He put the cap on it. We had a room full of people there. I'll never forget, Collins jumped up and said, "There's just some things you just can't push down an American's throat!" And Dean Hawkins let him get through, and then he leaned back and said, "Well, I'll tell you, Mr. Collins, Mr. Helstein and I and your union have agreed to a contract. The terms are all spelled out. As far as Armour is concerned, and I'm speaking for Armour, we intend to live by it. And I would suggest that if you feel that this is going to be something that you can't swallow and is going to be pushed down your throat, you have my permission right now to walk out that door and go down there to the plant and tell Mr. Hirschstein that I said to give you your time. You've got permission to do that, and you don't even have to come back. And anybody that feels the same way can do the same thing." Well, Collins sat down and we never heard nothing. He took his seat, and we never had another problem out of him.

In spite of the company's compliance with the new contract, local activists quickly discovered that the conventions of segregation were deeply ingrained amongst the union membership. Older habits of mind and action proved difficult to break.

Eddie Humphrey

Black workers were reluctant to do what we asked because this was something new. You had to have lived in that period of time to know what a black person had to go through under those segregated and discriminatory conditions. A lot were reluctant. Even after that partition had been moved out of the lunch room which separated the blacks from the whites sitting down eating, there were some blacks that would not go past that imaginary line because this was still in their minds.

Once Armour complied with the desegregation clause of the contract, local activists moved to overcome the problem of self-segregation.

Frank Wallace

We had a very divided situation at the time, but we did quite a job of education. The cafeteria thing, for instance, had to be done very slowly. You would talk with individual whites and individual blacks and get them to agree to go in and have lunch together. The same thing was true about the locker room thing. We would talk with those people who would be willing to move one to the other, and that's the way it began to develop. And then there was always some younger fellows there, both black, white, and Mexicans, a few of them were willing to be adventurous and do something. So we would get those people to join hands and go drink out of different fountains and all that kind of stuff that had previously been separated, you know, with the signs separating them. So that's the way we had to do it. It was a slow kind of thing; it wasn't done like a mad rush. We had blacks there who said, "No, I don't want to locker in their so-called white room," and the same with the whites saying no, they didn't want to go over to us. It wasn't easy, you know, because of all of the loud noises that were made by Mullins and his group.

L. C. Williams was one of the first activists chosen to break down self-segregation in the plant cafeteria. The white response was hostile but not especially violent.

L. C. Williams

We were encouraged by our leaders, locally and nationally, to try to usher this thing in, by refusing to go along with segregation in the lunch room— to get served, take a seat out there, and eat your food. Four or five of us from the loading dock, mostly the luggers like myself, we decided to take it on. We went through the line that served the whites, that was to try and help break this thing down, to point out to people that this was going to rub off on them and that I wasn't going to eat out of their plate. If it's the same food, well, what's wrong with everybody being served from the same place?

When I took my seat that first time, something—a banana peel or something—popped me on the back of the head. I didn't know where it came from, but one of the guys sitting in front of me said he thought he knew the guy that threw the peel. Well, I just sort of gave the guy a bitter look. We didn't create a scene there, with jobs involved and all, but that didn't happen again. Later on, I talked to the guy. Got him off in a corner and told him that I didn't appreciate it and thought that it was in very poor taste on his part, and that I wouldn't sit idly by again and see that happen. He apologized for it. He said, "You had a right to do what you were doing." So we bridged the gap; we healed some wounds.

Union leadership also attempted to persuade leading white and Mexican-American workers to move through the formerly "black" cafeteria line and sit with African Americans, thus setting a visible example for the rank-and-file membership.

Mary Salinas

We would go through the line, and after we got our tray, we made sure that some of us would stand on the opposite side—where the wall had existed at one time. We were called a lot of names due to that, but we didn't care. We had a job to do, and it for the best interest of the majority of the people.

Even as the situation inside the Fort Worth Armour was brought under control, the union faced a larger crisis in the form of a regional disaffiliation movement that shook packing locals across the South in 1953 and 1954. Although the key issue behind the rebellion was the UPWA's decision to move forward with plant desegregation, the dissidents cloaked their racism in a more acceptable anti-communist mantle and managed to temporarily secure powerful allies within the regional and national CIO. Embattled UPWA District Director Pittman cast his lot with the rebels, setting the scene for a tremendous internal battle.

In the end, several local unions—including two in Texas—disaffiliated from the UPWA. Significantly, these were locals whose memberships consisted almost exclusively of white workers. One of these, the Fort Worth stockyards local, was closely involved with the turmoil in the Armour plant. C. B. McCafferty's father, a founder of the stockyards local in the 1930s, vainly attempted to dissuade a younger generation of white stock handlers from leaving the UPWA and seeking refuge with the more conservative Amalgamated Meat Cutters. The "primeval appeal" of anti-communism mixed with racism proved too potent for him to combat.

C. B. McCafferty

He was still talking to them in the old ways, the old exhortations about solidarity, and these younger guys didn't have any idea what he was talking about. The only thing they knew was the Communists and niggers were coming in to take their jobs. It was a real hysteria and we were caught up in it.

African American workers, on the other hand, proved relatively impervious to the appeal of anti-communism. As McCafferty observed, "The blacks basically knew that it was a smokescreen for lack of progress in civil rights; they viewed anti-communism as a negative force." Time and again, black unionists confirmed this view. Often they elaborated by situating the abortive Red scare in the context of Texas in the mid-1950s.

Frank Wallace

What the hell, we didn't know nothing about Communism! You didn't have all the media that you got now back then. Everybody didn't have a TV to look at the evening news, and everybody wasn't able to buy a newspaper. So Communism wasn't the big bad wolf like it was in some of the eastern states or even around Chicago. It didn't catch on like wildfire like Pittman and his group thought it would. It wasn't a Red disease or cancer around here.

The rebellion fizzled out, and with it faded Director Pittman's hope of retaining power in the southwestern district. In 1954, George Thomas ran against him and defeated Pittman by a significant margin. The first black man to be elected to such a post in the South, Thomas enjoyed the support of most of the district's white workers. His election facilitated the efforts of union activists to combat long-standing discriminatory practices in hiring and promotion, such as the exclusion of African American women from sliced bacon. Opal Barner was the first black woman to exercise her seniority rights to transfer into this department.

Eddie Humphrey

When she bumped in, all of the white women decided to walk out and left her there, and she was sitting there crying. I was the chief steward of that division, so someone called me, and I went down to see what was wrong. The foreman there was named Alton, I never will forget him! Since all the other women walked out, and he was a part of their conspiracy, he wanted her to punch out her time card. I got there just in time. I said, "Opal, what are you doing?" She said, "Well, he told me punch out." I said, "Put that card down, let him punch it!" So I started talked to him. He said, "Well, I don't have anything for her to do." And I said, "That's your problem. Opal Barner bumped in here according to the agreement we have with your national people, and she's going to stay here. Now if you haven't got anything for her to do that's your business, you know, just as long as you pay her eight hours. If you're not going to pay her eight hours, she will go home." I said to Opal, "You stay right here, I don't want to hear no more crying out of you, and you stay right there. I don't care what Alton said, you stay on right here in this department. It's up to him to find something for you to do." So she saw I was serious. Well I got that taken care of.

Then I went down to the union hall. This was a big walkout. So when I walked in, oh boy, they knew who I was. George Thomas and I, we got on the phone and got in touch with a guy by the name of Hedges—he was the industrial-relation man for Armour and Company in Chicago. And sure enough, Hedges said, "Well, I'll call the superintendent, and if it went down like you said, then I'm going to give those women an ultimatum that if they're not back on the job in an hour's time, they can pick their paychecks up." So George told me to go out there and tell the women that. I said, "Ladies, I'm going to tell you all something. You've got two choices: as a matter of fact, you've got about fifty minutes to get back up there and get on your jobs, or your paychecks will be waiting for you. I don't care whether you work or not. There's not one of you out here can't be replaced. I don't care how many years [seniority] you have. You all know that the agreement is the youngest person in the plant be bumped, and this is what we're doing.

Opal Barner has been laid off out of her department. There are younger women in the plant that she has a right to bump, and we don't care whether she is black, brown, blue, polka-dot, or what. She has that right because her seniority entitled her to this." I wasn't nasty about it. I just told them what was told to me by the International office. Shit! Those women sat there and looked at each other for about two or three minutes. They weren't getting no support, so then they started trying to talk to George Thomas. George said, "Well, look now, your divisional steward has told you, your time is growing near; if I were you I would get on up there on the job. I don't have no more to say." And, man, in about a couple of more seconds, zoom, zoom, zoom! Now that was the first black bumping into a white department.

Those women found out that the custom that they had been used to, of treating blacks the way that they had done in the past, it was coming to an end. After that, I had a number of those same women that were involved in that walkout say, "Eddie, I was wrong, but I don't want you to tell nobody. I can work with anybody. All I want is my job." So, they realized then that there was a change.

Equally important to the gains made in Fort Worth in this period was winning white support for the elimination of discrimination. This was a difficult and, at times, complicated task. Activists found that when trying to persuade reluctant whites to support desegregation, an appeal to their material interests often succeeded.

L. C. Williams

We would point out to them that just because you was getting twenty cents more than I was getting for the same work, really, it wasn't anything to pat yourself on the back or beat your chest about—that this was just another one of the things that the company was using to make money off both of us. And in fact, they probably would tell you when you was getting that increase, don't tell so-and-so, you know, knowing that you was just as much entitled to it as the guy that he's giving it to because you're doing the same work, you're producing the same amount of work, and the product that you produce is passing inspection—it's just as good as anybody else's, but the thing is the color of your skin. I would say to them, "You know, as long as this company can keep this kind of thing between us and keep it going, and you support it, then we're never going to get this company on a solid front." It's just as simple as that. Not only were you suffering, but I was suffering. Now I was probably suffering more but—and this is what I would say to them—you're suffering too, because we both could get more if we eliminated this thing. If we erased it from our midst, we would probably both get more in benefits and wages alike.

116

So this is the sort of thing that I know that I personally used to try and persuade people to come around. I could see the thing they was doing to us. I certainly wasn't being helped by segregation, but the guy that was enjoying a little bit more, he was always afraid and then looking over his shoulder, see, because the company was constantly reminding him.

The changed atmosphere in the Fort Worth UPWA allowed packinghouse workers to register other gains in the mid- and late 1950s. The union pushed its civil rights activities beyond the confines of the plant and into the larger community, forging ties with the local branch of the NAACP and forcing the integration of the downtown Holden Hotel. It joined with other groups to desegregate Tarrant County's public schools and played a visible role protesting the brutal 1955 lynching of Emmett Till.

However, in 1959 Armour began scaling back its operations in Fort Worth and permanently closed the plant in 1963. This was part of a national restructuring of the meat industry, which ultimately decimated the UPWA. In 1968, the weakened union merged with its longtime rival, the Amalgamated Meat Cutters. A dramatic change in practice and style accompanied the merger.

Frank Wallace

There was a difference, quite a bit of difference. Some of the style and some of the method of doing reports were very much different. Some of the methods of negotiating was different, methods of organizing was different. I had a rough time trying to adjust to what the new setup was and what it required. Instead of having a large committee from the local group [in negotiations], you might only have the business agent and maybe one individual from the local, which was completely different from our method of negotiating. It was something new to us; we hadn't been accustomed to this kind of thing. We had been used to the people having more input as to the negotiations, to their grievances, to their settlements.

In 1979 the Meat Cutters merged again, this time with the Retail Clerks, to form the United Food and Commercial Workers (UFCW), now the largest affiliate of the AFL-CIO.

It was just about as much change as with the first merger, maybe a little bit more so. To me, it seemed that we had moved from being a labor organization to becoming a small corporation of some type ourselves. You don't have very much input on how things are going to be done; you found out how they want you to do them and you do them. Here again our reporting was different: we used to report every two weeks; you changed and give reports every week. Past instances where it might have been appropriate for you to print your report, now you must type your report. It must be very neat. You've got to have so many hours to make out your report; you can't make it out in three or four. You've got so many paragraphs that's got to be in your report.

In most cases that you're working on, you must have on a tie and a coat, regardless of whether you are working in a temperature of 100 or 110 degrees. There are a lot of differences from one organization to the other; there's a lot of things that come down that has no bearing on the job that you do, or the job that you are expected to do whatsoever, you know. If I'm working servicing a poultry house, I look like a fool going in there with a tie on, and a pair of fifty-dollar shoes when I should have on some four-dollar shoes from Kmart or something like that you know. And I've got to take a visit to that chicken slime and stuff and to visit my people inside of the poultry house. I'm old-fashioned about the labor movement. I don't think we should become too modern to the extent that we're going be like General Motors. We represent the employees of General Motors, but let's not become like the corporate headquarters.

Despite his dismay over the deterioration of packinghouse unionism in recent years, Wallace and other activists derived a sense satisfaction from the accomplishments of the UPWA and the role that they played in improving packinghouse workers' lives.

I think that I was able to help some of the employees that I had to handle grievances for, negotiate contracts for, handle arbitration cases for. I hope that I was able to help them to the extent of making their lives a little bit better in the workforce. If it was nothing but getting them a few more pennies per hour, or making their job a little easier, or getting them some additional benefits, that would help them and their families when they reach retirement age, or if they happened to have a family of kids and illness occurred, I hope that I was able to help negotiate a contract that would supply them with adequate hospitalization and sick-leave benefits, this kind of thing.

I gained a heck of satisfaction of knowing that I have been able to help somebody some of the time. It's the satisfaction that comes within you. It's not a monetary value, but it's a pleasing satisfaction you get. I felt good about being able to get some guy back to work that was discharged, that I felt was discharged unjustly. I felt good about getting a guy's suspension lifted that might have been for six weeks and I got him only two weeks and he was back to work. I felt good if I was able to get some guy a few more pennies for his work where the boss had cheated him out of it. So, it's the kind of feeling which you get. It's a wonderful feeling, to know that you've been able to help somebody.

6

"LOOKING FOR THE PROMISED LAND"
Labor and Civil Rights in Waterloo, Iowa

At first glance, Waterloo, Iowa, might seem an unusual place for black workers to make up a significant portion of the packinghouse workforce. Located on the Cedar River in northern Iowa, Waterloo's Rath plant was one of many packinghouses built in the corn belt in the 1890s. Like its better-known neighbor to the north, George A. Hormel & Co. in Austin, Minnesota, (located on the same river), Rath was a family concern that specialized in pork products. Founded in 1891, Rath grew slowly until demand for cured and canned pork products accelerated following the First World War. Rath increased its capacity for manufacturing processed foods such as sausage and bacon in the 1920s and modernized its pork operations in the 1930s. Rath became Iowa's largest packinghouse when it built a large beef killing and processing operation during World War II. By the mid-1950s there were more than five thousand workers at the plant. In union parlance, Rath was one of the "big independents" that were able to compete effectively against the large national firms of Armour, Cudahy, Swift, and Wilson.

The large African American presence in Waterloo can be traced to efforts by the Illinois Central railroad to break a strike of white union members in the 1910s. The company recruited black strikebreakers in Mississippi, and the men stayed on afterward and brought their families to town. The black population jumped from only 24 in 1910 to 837 in 1920 and grew steadily thereafter through natural increase and slow but steady migration from Mississippi and declining coal towns in southern Iowa. World War II accelerated black population growth, as a new wave of migrants came to Waterloo in search of, as Jimmy Porter remembered, "the promised land." By 1950, there were 2,587 blacks in Waterloo, 4 percent of the city's population.

Waterloo accepted the black presence grudgingly. Although racial discrimination technically violated Iowa law, it was widespread. Restrictive covenants and the informal practices of realtors restricted blacks to a small residential district sharply circumscribed by the tracks of the Illinois Central and two

119

other railroad lines. Blacks faced widespread discrimination in public accommodations, restaurants, and recreation facilities. Black women found employment only as custodians or domestics, and men were limited to laboring and portering jobs in those businesses that would hire them. As in other Midwestern cities, jobs in meatpacking were among the best available for blacks even though they were restricted to only a few departments in the Rath plant.

Blacks were an integral part of the local union, which secured certification in the early 1940s. Increasing black presence in the plant after World War II and the UPWA's 1948 strike transformed the local union into a dynamic and militant organization. In 1948, packinghouse workers rioted when black strikebreaker Fred Lee Roberts shot and killed white union member Chuck Farrell on the picket line. It is noteworthy that the riot was directed solely against the Rath company and not Waterloo's black community. The National Guard suppressed the rioting and subsequently allowed the company to bring strikebreakers into the plant. As company-union relations deteriorated in the aftermath of the strike defeat, the growing number of black workers at Rath were able to link their grievances against racial discrimination with Local 46's more confrontational stance toward management. In the mid-1950s, black workers were able to use Local 46 as a springboard to attack established patterns of discrimination in the community.

Robert Burt

Robert Burt was born in Waterloo in 1922 as one of eight children. His father came north to work on the Illinois Central railroad during a strike. A minister in Mississippi before moving to Iowa, Burt's father started a church in his new home and later served as a deacon. Robert himself became a minister in 1960.

Robert Burt's brothers and sisters all spent time working for the Rath Packing Company. His brother Percy was a minister and an important founder of UPWA Local 46, and his sister Ada Tredwell was one of the first black women to hold a production job at Rath. Robert Burt started in the plant's hog kill department in 1941 and immediately became a union steward. He spent 1942 to 1946 in the military and returned to the hog kill afterward. Burt resumed his union activities, subsequently serving as assistant divisional steward and divisional steward in the hog kill. In 1960, Burt was elected chairman of the local's Human Rights Committee. He retired in 1983. In addition to membership in Local 46, Burt was also active in the Mount Calvary Baptist Church, the Masons, and the NAACP.

Our family is a religious family. I grew up in church. Everybody, everybody in Waterloo knew the Burts. If any of our kids did anything, well, they didn't do nothing, just called home and that was it.

[My father] built the church that's known in Waterloo as the Union Baptist Church, and when I say built, I mean didn't have the big machine to dig out the holes for the basement. There was four boys, and the rest of the men in the church, we dug out the basement by hand, and then lay the blocks. After he left there, he built another church out in Maywood. I started pastoring out to that church, and then in 1980 I was called to a church in town here called the Mount Calvary Baptist Church.

In an area to the east—what we call Highland—the only time they had blacks over there was cleaning up the houses and yards, but as far as moving in that area, it was out of the question. When I moved here it was all white, I was the first black family. As soon as I bought this house, well, being a black family coming in, the signs went on this side and across the street. Everybody was wanting to move out.

There was a lot of places that you could cook in but you couldn't eat in. When I was going to school there used to be a place called Jakes, and we would go there in the back and eat all we want to eat, but we couldn't come in the front and sit down at the table and eat. That's the way it was down South, and the same thing here in Waterloo. It didn't bother us so much because we didn't have the money to go down to the store anyhow. It was invisible as far as us concerned, the racial issue, because you just accept so much. Later you realize that a lot of things that you ought to have you don't have; then you start fighting for them.

In the small town of Waterloo, the Rath plant was a major source of employment for blacks. For those with roots in the town, it was routine for relatives to work there. One family member's good work record could help others get jobs.

I started working in the hog kill department on what we call the scalding tubs. I think Russell Lasley [elected UPWA vice president in 1948] got hired two or three days after I did. They drop them in the tub and then we had poles to bring them up the tub and put them in the scraper.

Just about all my family worked there at one time or another. Somebody recommend you, like a superintendent, he knew my brother and eventually he knew me. I don't think it was anything as far as the family, because they wanted people that's going to work every day, and I just didn't believe in taking off.

Forty-three years I cannot recall I took a day off, just took a day off, like some guys do, and didn't have until the last ten years that I took off sick. No, I just couldn't go in for that, never did. Because first thing is, I had a family, and next thing is, I like things, and you have to work if you want nice things. And so I always did, I like nice things, I like to have money in my pocket. On top of that, I was church-going, and I like to pay money into the church. So, I just worked all the time. I ain't saying that I didn't have a headache, or something like that and didn't feel like going, but I feel obligated. I believe in working.

Along with his older brother Percy, Burt was active in the initial organizing drive at Rath just before he entered the military.

When I went in it wasn't organized. "CIO," a guy named Ackerson, was one of the main guys in keeping this together. He had a kind of a unity going where we were sticking together. He was somewhat more familiarized with the CIO, that's the reason why we called him that. The tactics he brought there and put into use let us know he must have been familiarized with organizing the union. A lot of times things pertained to safety, job loads, and racial stuff, he knew something about. He showed us the ropes.

He used that knowledge, and with a group of us, the hog kill department being the strong department, the guys got together. A lot of them jobs anybody couldn't do, and so they couldn't kick them off the job. The hog kill was tough, right. It was my department, I admit, we was the toughest thing going; we was known throughout the whole state of Iowa, Rath packinghouse. [laughing]

I was pretty well familiarized with organizations. Practically all my life I was an organizer, so, I just fell in line. We started passing out buttons, and wasn't even fully organized. I helped pass out buttons. Some of them hesitated taking them, because they didn't want to be known, but we did it anyhow.

We take this position, that you being in the union you've got somebody to fight for you. A lot of times guys think you can go along without the union, and he finds that once the foreman fire you, then being out of the union, there isn't nobody to protect you. So this was one of the persuasive methods that we used, is to get them in the union, so you can have your protection that you're supposed to have.

Point we put across is that you have seniority, and you have this right. A lot of time, being black you didn't have too many rights. I know several cases where a black could have got a job but didn't get it till the union came in. Most of the guys that came at the packinghouse went to the lower job, you know, like the scalding tub in the hog. When they go upstairs, well then, that's where most of the white guys worked.

Charles Pearson

Charles Pearson was born in Waterloo, Iowa, on June 17, 1925. Pearson's father had moved with his family to Waterloo from Mississippi. He was recruited by the Illinois Central to break a strike of white railroad workers. Pearson first worked with his brothers shining shoes and later as a busboy at a downtown hotel.

Like Robert Burt, Charles Pearson began working at Rath during World War II. But Pearson, by his own admission, tended to take a "radical stand" and became a central figure in a militant current inside Local 46. In alliance with white leftists "CIO" Ackerson and Lowell Hollenbeck, Pearson and his supporters among younger black workers stimulated confrontational shop-floor behavior and aggressive civil rights activity.

I was working at the Russell Campson Hotel. I was made the head busboy, and when they made me head busboy, I thought that everybody should get a raise. I called the busboys and two of the waiters together, and told them they should get more money, because I got a dollar raise. It got to the chef and he called me down and asked me, what did I mean about a raise. They didn't have a union there and he didn't want no union to talk with. It angered me, so I called everybody together and said I got a dollar raise and I think everybody should get a raise. Five of the busboys and two of the waitresses were with me one hundred percent. We said, before lunch is a good time to get your raise, nobody will go to work. So we didn't go to work. No water on the table, no forks, anything, on the table. The chef runs upstairs and I was fired. It was a favor in a sense. The people there got their raise. I got fired, and that's when I was called to the packinghouse.

I went to work in October '42. At that time, the union was still mediocre. You didn't get the drive that you heard that the unions gave.

Charles Pearson, 1986. *Photo by Rick Halpern.*

123

Punchy ["CIO"] Ackerson always talked union. You may not have heard of him, he may be low-key, but he wasn't low-key, he was the person I looked upon. He would come to me and tell me blacks should be more involved into the union, because if they were more involved it would make the union stronger, and would do more for blacks.

Punchy had me study union people, John L. Lewis, and Walter Reuther. As I studied them, he was telling me about a consolidation between black and white. "Why can't you go over there and have a beer? Why can't you go over and have a sandwich?"

After approximately four months, Punchy arranged for me to be a shop steward. I went to both of my brothers—both of them were packinghouse workers—and told them that Punchy wanted me to be a steward. They told me it was up to myself. So I became a steward. In the resin [room] there were three stewards, none black, and they make me that fourth steward.

They called these nigger jobs at the time—the resin room, driving hogs, sticking or the tubs. Guys were pretty roughshod, like Punchy; Punchy was a rough person who didn't take anything off of anybody.

After I obtained the steward I moved up on the inner floor. I left and went to the military about that time.

Pearson's experiences in the segregated military during World War II reinforced his inclination toward militancy.

I was all enthused about going to the military for the simple reason in the military we don't have to worry about discrimination. That's the first time I confronted racism, when I was in uniform, that I knew was racism as people talk about it. I couldn't understand, I'm in uniform, and I can't go on this street or that street. I felt as though, coming back from the military, I wouldn't have to meet this concept any more, of this one's for black and this one's for white. Other than that, my military experience gave me the initiative to do what I did in the union; the strategies used in the military were some of the same strategies and techniques that we used in the union. You were aggressive enough, and while you're under aggression you stay under aggression, and you got the opposition tilted, and you keep 'em tilted, and if you keep 'em tilted you can win.

I was in two racial confrontations, one in Florida and another one in Virginia. The first one was in McDale Field, Florida. A mulatto or octoroon black lady came to the base to see her husband. When she came to the base the military police stopped her for the simple reason they thought she was white. This started a confrontation between the white military and the black soldiers. We ran into the racial thing at Savannah, and they were talking about sending the First Cavalry in to break it up. We lowered 105s and 155s on Savannah, and said if they send the First Cavalry in, we was going to shell the town. They pulled us out and shipped us into Virginia. I was on an army base, and they had a racial break between the navy and the army there.

Most of it was fisticuffs, knives or something like that, until we got back on base. They had a lot of small arms there, and the guys, not knowing what happened, would go to firing.

It gave me the status of saying, it's easy to obtain if you fight for it.

Immediately after the war, Pearson returned to Rath and quickly reestablished links with Punchy Ackerson and his ally, Lowell Hollenbeck. This group expanded over the next few years to challenge more moderate union leaders, such as Robert Burt, and to push for more militant tactics by Local 46.

I learned when I was overseas, leading was having a following. If you win you have a following; if you lose you don't. Mine was always from a radical stand. Shut off the chain, shut it off and you get it. That was Hollenbeck's teaching.

Lowell Hollenbeck came in '46, '47. A lot of times they got to thinking Hollenbeck was a plant, someone had sent him in, maybe from the International, to organize and get the plant working as a hard-core union. He said, "You guys are not unionized; you're not doing as unions do." He pulled the weight from the leadership that was in the beginning.

Lowell was a guy that never quit. Let's go! Let's find something to do, everything can't be just okeydokey! Punchy worked very strongly with Hollenbeck, because they used the same kind of strategies. Those people were always trying to put something in contention, if they could find it.

Hollenbeck came in, and he salt and peppered us around. It started in the woods. We would go in the woods, and we would sit around and we would talk. He would say, "I'm going to make you a foreman, I'm going to make you a divisional steward. Chuck, I'm going to make you chairman of anti-discrimination," which we didn't have at the time. Within a period of six weeks, he had brought this about.

Lowell Hollenbeck would salt and pepper meetings. I would be sitting here, you would be sitting there, and he would be sitting over there. Maybe eight of us would be situated within the crowd. I get up and say, "Well, I'm in opposition of this," and somebody say, "Yeah, that's right," and they go to clapping. Pretty soon the old guard would have to confirm with the rank-and-file body, and the rank-and-file body was making the noise. It would be four, five people that would start that.

My brother and Reverend Burt didn't like the techniques we were using. But they went along because we had ways of shutting that chain down, and everyone had to shut down. They began to give us the cooperation we needed. We came to coincide with each other, where before they would draw back when you go to talk about walking out or stopping the chain.

As Pearson indicated, the militancy of his group did eventually influence Robert Burt and other established union leaders who found combative shop-floor tactics an effective way to overcome company resistance. As a central union leader, Burt was well positioned to observe the endemic conflict with management over day-to-day workplace issues. Militancy by the local union included the use of job actions that technically violated the contract.

Robert Burt

Chuck Pearson was a steward, a type of troubleshooter. He worked mostly on the hog kill on the night shift dealing with the radical type of person. He had leadership capacity. He helped out the union as far as the second shift were concerned. He was in many situations where people would get fired and tried to get the people their job back. You might call him radical, of course, go sometimes to the extreme. He had people back behind. They thought of him as a leader. So he played a big part in the union.

They had three shifts. When things are going on, like a stoppage, we would be involved, because if they have a stop or they get suspended, it would be up to the first shift to support them. Some of the foremen weren't too good, their attitude was to drive people, or to try to make a name for themselves. So Chuck had to combat all of this.

When I was a head steward there, I tried to talk with the personnel or the foremen and see if can try and get things settled. Then if we don't come to no agreement, well then I call four or five stewards out, and we try to negotiate the interpretation of the contract. Sometimes we were asking for leniency on some individual that missed three days out of a week, excessive absenteeism, which companies don't appreciate. We try to negotiate with the person and the company; the person to try not to be absent, and the company to take him back. If the person got fifteen or twenty years there and was worth saving, well then we might go to an attitude of slowing down, letting the company know that they're not getting the hogs in the cooler that they ought to get. Then if that don't work, the other alternative is a walkout. Usually we walk out and leave all the hogs hanging just there, and some cases where the walkout is not to the extent, we take all the hogs off the rail then walk out. Usually when we walk out with all the hogs on the rail, the foremens and superintendent got to come up and clean them off, because the inspector don't allow them so long to hang up there.

We would try and get all these departments with stewards and meet and see the problem that they had. Well we want everybody out, we don't want no department to get caught out there on a limb by themself.

I'm not too well pleased to go begging somebody. I didn't like it much but I would go through with it, to try to save a person. A lot of times you know in your mind that it's very hard to change the person, once he got absenteeism record like he had, yet still you keep begging and getting him back on the job. We tried to circulate our stewards around to get the attitude of the people. I don't say well heck no, he ain't worth saving, but we tried to save a person who was good. Then we get the attitude of the people, we go to the company and demand that this guy be placed back, and usually he gets put back, but he'll lose hours or get two or three days off. But he's still got a job.

Jimmy Porter

The militant approach of Pearson's group coincided with a demographic shift in the workforce, as many black southerners moved to Waterloo during and immediately after the Second World War. Jimmy Porter exemplified the high expectations of this cohort of union members. Porter was born in Holmes County, Mississippi, in 1931. His mother was a domestic worker, and a cousin in Tunica, Mississippi, raised Porter and his seven brothers. In 1948, Porter moved to Waterloo and found employment at the local John Deere plant. In 1954, Rath hired Porter, and he went to work in the resin room on the hog kill. He quickly became active in the local union and was elected trustee in 1955. He later served as divisional steward, financial secretary, and as vice president. Porter played a key role in the union's

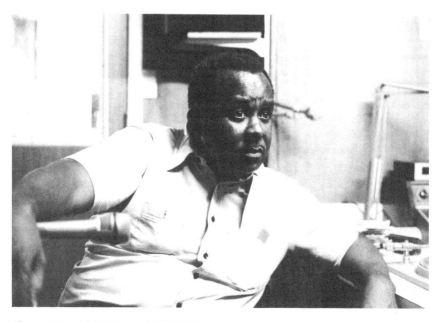

Jimmy Porter, 1986. *Photo by Rick Halpern.*

anti-discrimination activities and was an important leader in Waterloo's civil rights struggles through the 1960s. In 1973, he left Rath to launch a community-based African American radio station, KBBG.

I came to Waterloo the last part of 1948, looking for the promised land. I wasn't quite eighteen years of age and I had been told that if I could only come to the Midwest that this was the land of opportunity, and all I had to do was to work. I discovered that the land was here but the promises were little different from those I had just left. Let me hasten to add they were different. It wasn't as obvious, or as pronounced, or as blatant as it was in Mississippi. I pretty well knew where I stood in Mississippi and here I had to be told and reminded.

The other thing that was so discouraging to me was how well they had domesticated their black people. They had conditioned most of the blacks who lived here to never look at how well they should be doing compared to whites who they had gone to school with, but to measure themselves by their country cousin, those of us coming up from the southland. It was amazing how well they taught them to measure themselves versus another black person in order to feel good about themself.

Black southerners like Porter were inclined to follow Pearson rather than the moderate leadership drawn from established Waterloo blacks. Accordingly, Pearson's group made a special effort to bring the southerners into influential union positions.

Charles Pearson

Shortly after the war probably eighty-five percent of the kill would have been southerners. Now, the old guard, like my brother, Reverend Burt, they were substantial Waterlooians. The people that came to work with me, Jimmie and O. C. Smith and all, were out of the South.

O. C. Smith worked heads, a very essential job on the killing floor. O. C. had come up from the South, and he had a good following, most of the guys. He was a big strapping young man, and had a reputation of being a little rough. The guys in the shackling pen, on the tub, and the drivers, was mostly Southerners, so he could stop them at a given time. So we put a steward badge on O. C.

They seem to have enjoyed the thing of union; the union said that we have this coming. They fell right in cycle with the radical status of it. Out of the breakup the '48 strike, they knew that the company was really out to break the union.

The 1948 strike acted as a training school in militant tactics for the new cohort of black union members. Tense picket line confrontations during the strike climaxed in the murder of white union member Chuck Farrell by a black strikebreaker in front of the Rath plant. The National Guard entered Waterloo to suppress subsequent rioting by union members and supporters.

If there was a racial break, it would have been at that time: a black man killing a white man. It never got to the point that someone said, he killed Chuck Farrell because he was white, or because the black man is getting ready to cross the picket line.

They would line the police up, both sides, letting you in if you want to come in. The "goon squad," we called them, came down from St. Paul, and brings in half a truckload of ax handles, and they carries us to a type of drill. The police are there but they can't pull those weapons; all they've got is their stick. Now here's your stick, and your stick. We utilize that to the point that we didn't come into combat with the police, but the police couldn't do anything to really control the masses on the street. This is where they pulled the National Guard in. And when they pulled the Guards in, we knew ax handles was out of the question, because you've got a .50 calibre machine gun on top of the building and you've got a half track running up and down Sycamore. Even at this point, it seemed like the people in the street drew closer together, the black and the white unified. Like, well hell, we're going to lose our jobs if we don't combine and stay together.

The only complaint that I felt was I lost some material things. But if it hadn't have been, we wouldn't have achieved what we have now. That pulled us back, saying if you're going to be here within this plant, you are going to be union, and if you're not going to be union, you can't be within this plant.

The UPWA's 1948 strike was a watershed for Local 46. The bruising conflict with the company on the picket line, and bitter union-management conflicts in the strike's aftermath, stimulated both shop-floor militancy and civil rights activity. Blacks made determined efforts to move into departments previously dominated by whites. When blacks encountered resistance, the union took care to place the blame on the company for maintaining lily-white departments, and contended that job actions designed to compel desegregation inside the plant were directed against management, not other workers.

Robert Burt

The company came back in with the whip, like they were in the forties. Because in the forties, you wasn't even allowed to go to a rest room, wasn't

National Guardsmen keep Local 46's headquarters shut following the riot that erupted when a black strikebreaker killed a white striker. *Used with permission of the State Historical Society of Wisconsin [WHi (X3) 50372].*

allowed to have time off to go to smoke; the only time you had was your dinner hour. Back then the foreman had the whip, he can do what he wanted to do, and he did what he wanted to do, and you was somewhat a slave, because you either did it or you in front of the plant. A lot of cases where the person had to go to the bathroom, he wouldn't let him go, and he ended up in a bladder condition, and kidney conditions. Then when the '48 strike came, it reverted back to about the same thing; although we had a union, it wasn't like it was in the forties. The foreman had the whip.

The only thing that got them by was the union. If the union wasn't in there, well, it really would have been like it was before the union was organized.

The '48 strike opened some doors for the blacks. [Before the strike] as far as the black male, they were confined to the hog kill and the sheep kill and the beef kill; even in some of them departments they was confined to a lower part of the work. I know. I don't have to speculate on that, I went through it.

The '48 strike actually broke loose just about everything, and all the departments that was all white, well then the blacks started moving into them departments. You got the seniority, and the company went along with it. We had a great influx of black male and female who had seniority, and that seniority moved them right up the line. They went in a department and the people had to accept them if they wanted a job. Years prior to that, it wasn't open but to certain people that knew it was open, and they would transfer in and out. When it got wide open, then some of the blacks saw this as an opportunity to go in, and so they infiltrated these places, and then if they can weather the storm well then they're all right. But I never left the hog kill; I stayed in that department forty-three years.

Before, the company would hesitate letting you go in there, and the union had to take a grievance to get that person in. Then once you got in, then you're fighting against your own union members, 'cause they didn't want you in there. So long as you ain't in there, well you're buddy-buddy, but once you go in there, you find this hatred arise.

The company wanted the work to come out, and they didn't move unless they had to. So after the '48 strike we made them move. After that, well then they say they wouldn't work, they hit the street, and that changed their attitude, 'cause a lot of 'em had good jobs, especially in the bacon and the mechanical.

The mechanical department down there was one of the main ones opened up. A job opened up and the guys bid, and he go down there. The mechanics didn't want him, but they couldn't do nothing about it. Like everything else, you get your seniority, and so we had the blacks in top jobs.

The bacon was all lily-white; I don't think even the janitor come in there. The '48 strike opened up everything, and so when Ada Tredwell and three other black females got in the bacon, they [white women] walked out. When they walked out, well then the hog kill department sympathized with [the black women] and shut down. It was a walkout, it wasn't no strike, it was just a walkout, protest. So the company come to the conclusion that if you guys didn't want to work then you would be replaced, and so then they all came back to work.

Electricians didn't have no blacks until way after the '48 strike. Before I left, they had a black female in that department. She happened to be my niece. She was a type that was energetic, and she wanted to learn and did learn. Sometimes I see her carrying all them bags of tools around her waist, and I wonder how she walked. But a black female in that department—it shows you how far they came after the '48 strike.

We had a lot of problems, not only with the worker but with the foremen, until people realized that people wanted to go where they want, the seniority let them go, and they had to accept it. You had this attitude, this biased attitude on who you wanted to work, who you wanted to do that. It never did get cleared up even over this period of years. But they just kept on, in the electric shop and the carpenters shop and the plumbing, all them, people just kept flowing in there. The attitude of some never did change, but they couldn't stop the flow, and so a lot of the departments opened up.

We did several things. We called the foreman and told them that this person don't want to be harassed, and we don't want the people to do anything against this person here, and hold the foreman responsible. We talk with the people, and then we had a department meeting. You find some die hard; well the time's gone, you know, and so we had to put that across, and lay down what's what. Then we instruct the foremens to carry out what was supposed to be carried out. Now as far as a department like bacon, we didn't slow down or stop because of the people; we did that because the company didn't do their job. We take the attitude, that's up to the company to carry out. But as far as union against union, we didn't take that type of attitude.

Ada Tredwell

One of the key figures breaking down discrimination against black women at Rath was Burt's older sister, Ada Tredwell. She was born in Taylor, Mississippi, in 1916 and moved to Waterloo later that year. After completing high school, Tredwell worked at custodial and domestic jobs. In 1941, she began working as a janitor at Rath. Tredwell became active in Local 46 in the early 1950s and was one of the first black women to transfer into production jobs in the plant.

We were just coming out of the Depression, and jobs were very scarce for everyone, but for black women there was nothing hardly, except domestic or custodial kinds of jobs. Jobs for black women at that time were very scarce.

I was hired at Rath in 1941, and at that time they had three black women. They were janitors. It was terrible, the work we had to do. We were supervised by a matron who was dedicated to Rath's, everything had to be just so. We took care of all the ladies' rest rooms and we also had to take care of halls and stairways. Sometimes we would have to go in at four o'clock in the morning in order to mop and scrub the offices, because we were unable to do it in the daytime. At that time they didn't have machines like they do now that do all this scrubbing and waxing. You had to do it on your hands and knees, and that was a long, long night, on your hands and knees, going over these offices. [laughing] I think about it sometimes and I think, oh God, how we worked! You would go over it first on your hands and knees with soap and water, and then you would have to go back over it on your hands and knees with wax. Then we had to climb high on ladders to do all the windows and blinds.

When I started we were getting twelve dollars and fifty cents a week. It was more money, because I was getting five dollars a week doing house-work, but the work was an increase also. We worked every day except Sunday, and sometimes on Sunday.

At that time the union was not for us. We didn't really feel it like the fellows did. A majority of the people working participated, but the men really spearheaded that movement.

One reason the union could make such great inroads as fast as they did, the company did not have a lot of people who were loyal. Most people had beefs that had not been solved, and the company was very high-handed in their dealing with people. I think that was one of the greatest reasons why people felt like a union is what we need, because this company cares nothing about us.

We knew the reason we were janitors and not bacon slicers or something was because we were black. That was always one of the big arguments, was this going to be our lot for the rest of our lives, or did you really want to do something better. In 1940 that was pretty much like the way it was over the country; there was not a lot of clamor for black women being promoted to different kinds of jobs. That was what was expected, and this is your lot, so accept it.

Some people were satisfied with the way it was, but when you look at other people who make more money than you do, work less hours than you do, and work not nearly as hard, you just can't be happy. You just compare it all the time. It was our lot at the time, but there were some of us who were not happy with it. When we would go to a union meeting, our thing was, how come we could not work in the plant.

The black men wanted us out of there. We would be out there scrubbing steps with a scrub brush, and it would be break time for them, and the men would come through, and . . . oh, terrible! They wanted us out of there, and given the same kind of opportunity that other women had. They didn't want to see us climbing high up on ladders, doing all those kind of things that men should have been doing in the first place. That was before women's liberation! At that time women were still treated different than men. So there was a real push with the black union members to equalize the kinds of jobs that black women done and white women done.

When they finally decided that black women could work in the plant, you first had to be on the janitor and then go from there into the plant; you could not be hired off the street and go into the plant.

I can remember the day we signed up for the union. We joined, and then we decided we would apply. If you wanted to work in the plant you had to say what department you wanted to work in, then wait for an opening. The union said why don't you apply for the casing department, because they're going to have some openings in there soon. So we did; I started in casing.

There was two or three of us that went in at that time, and the department was about thirty or forty people, mostly women. Sometimes while we were on janitor, we made friends. When you go out in the plant and clean rest rooms, women would be in there, and you would just talk, and you make friends. Some of the friendliest of them were in casing, and we didn't have any real problems in there. Individually you might have had some problems, but as a department I don't think we had any.

What the employees will do or won't do depends on the policy of the company and how willing they are to enforce that policy. We transferred from casings to frozen foods. Frozen foods was really a nice department, you didn't get dirty. In casings, boy, you got wet and it was nasty. This one woman that was working with me told the boss that she didn't want to work with that nigger. By this time the union is pretty strong, and he told her, "Why don't you check out and go home." I never had any problems with her after that.

Three women who were hired off the street went into the bacon department, and the bacon department walked out. Rath said there was nothing they could do. What they really wanted to do was to fire the three black women. But the hog kill said that if you fire those women, then we are going to walk out also. In fact they just threatened to walk out; they just stopped working. That same day, Rath told the women in bacon, that they either go back to work or else they're fired. So that ended that.

I did have a great deal of respect for the union, because if it had not been for the union we would not have been in the plant. There's just no doubt about that. Before I left Rath, all the women were in the union, because there was just no way you cannot recognize what the union had done for us.

In a few years, the accomplishments of Tredwell and other black women to be able to transfer into the plant led to a fight for black women to be hired directly into production jobs without having to first work as janitors. Anna Mae Weems, already well known in the community, was one of ten black women recruited by Local 46 to break the company's resistance to hiring black women into production departments.

Anna Mae Weems

I was born and raised in Waterloo. My father played for Duke Ellington's band. My grandfather, Preston Hicky, used to work for a man called Casey Jones. I don't know if you heard the old legend about Casey Jones. In 1907 there were no blacks here in Waterloo and the whites were on strike here for more wages. So they went down to Water Valley, Mississippi and got my grandfather. Had a whole bunch of blacks on the train, brought them up

Anna Mae Weems, 1986. *Photo by Rick Halpern.*

here and said "now take over these jobs," and broke the strike. He came up here as an engineer. So we stayed, and I was born here. My mother died about four years after I was born, and my father couldn't find no work here. So he went to play trombone for Duke Ellington. Two years later the sister keeping us died. So he came back to get us.

When I graduated I couldn't understand why I—leader of the East High Band, played in the orchestra, could type, could swim—and I couldn't get any jobs here. I'd see the white girls I graduated with doing, and I couldn't get it. My dad, being out in the world, would explain to me about these things. I just started like that, as a need, that I know I should have had equal rights.

I was approached by Charles Pearson, Isadore Patterson, Chuck Durden, and a man named Hollenbeck. These were friends of mine, and they asked me if I would come in and take a test. I said "a test for what?", and they said "to pass a test that dealt with dexterity and some common knowledge." The test was to open up the doors for blacks to go into the packinghouse into a

135

department. Heretofore, blacks would have to mop and scrub before they could be moved into a department. The union was working on that, so they gave me this test, and I passed.

Somehow they knew I was coming when I passed the test. The girls wouldn't speak to me, they wouldn't let me have a out, you have to let each other outs. Took a man to let me out.

They thought that blacks shouldn't be in there, and they saw it as a threat to have black women coming in. They felt I didn't have a right to be in there. The scabs were better than me then.

I had to win these people, so what I did I sat on the brake. Making money, that's all they wanted to do, they just didn't want anyone to interfere with making money. Then to really make them like me I scooped pounds of bacon without even weighing it.

I got to be the divisional steward, then they needed me for everything.

Being their steward I was able to reason with them by degree. They needed me for their grievances, when a belt break down they wanted to make sure they get the next belt, and they wanted to make sure somebody protect their rights. I was the person to protect their rights. In fact, when I be out for a union activity maybe three or four times a week, they would complain about me being gone. They didn't like that, they only wanted what I could benefit them. It wasn't that they wanted me so much as just help them make money. They never really wholeheartedly accepted me.

Shop-floor bargaining and racial militancy resulted in the establishment of a powerful Human Relations/Civil Rights Committee in the Rath local (union members referred to it by both names). Its activism in the community often took place in alliance with the NAACP.

Robert Burt

We had a good Human Rights Committee. I got on it the later part of the years out there. In the forties the union was just beginning to come in. Then between '46 and '48 there wasn't too much involvement. I would have to say somewhere in the early fifties civil rights became more prominent, because the women wanted to be more involved in the union.

White women had bacon and other departments that were lily-white. They were making pretty good money, and they weren't too much concerned about women as a whole. They was more concerned about themselves. When the Civil Rights Committee begins, they take the attitude charity starts at home. They begin to work in the plant. So the women became involved because a lot of them wanted to move out of the janitorial department and go into a department of the plant where they could make more money and have better jobs. When they took this attitude, then women came more involved in the civil rights movement. The women became more active in the union. And not only that, women acted as officers of the union. When the Civil Rights Committee got to really function, Anna Mae Weems played an active part in the black women being moved where they want to move.

The Civil Rights Committee was about fifty-fifty sometimes. Most of the time there were more blacks on the committee. It got so high that a lot of times they wanted to cut some of the members off. At one time they had a committee for the morning and a committee for the night. Then the morning committee didn't think it was feasible to cut down the number of people, and so it went back to meeting together again. But meeting from both shifts, they had to pay the second shift for the time they had off from work to come to the meeting. I was chairman for about eleven or twelve years.

The committee was so active that we did work for John Deere's. John Deere never did have a civil rights committee, so they come to our committee seeking a solution to their problem, and then we sent out a task force. In fact, something in the community come up, it come to the Civil Rights Committee, and we give them direction. Somebody might have a problem at a grocery store, they come to our Human Rights Committee. We even dealt with the city of Waterloo. A lot of time, people just don't know, and we give them direction.

In the process of developing its own strong Human Rights Committee, the Rath local developed a strong working relationship with the local NAACP around civil rights issues.

Back in that time, you didn't have too many places that was open for blacks. A lot of times they can cook, but they couldn't eat. The restaurants wasn't too open. A lot of times a guy, he had to pay a hundred dollar fine, but he would go back to the same thing. And a lot of times people have a general attitude that they just don't go to those places. They could go but they don't go because they hadn't been brought up that way. Well, the NAACP opened up a lot of these places.

At that time, the Ten Cents Store, Woolworth, and places like that didn't hire no blacks. Well, then we didn't buy and let the people know what we were doing. The other alternative, we gather around the place on the outside and have signs saying, "This place is discriminating."

We had a couple of stores that didn't want to hire the blacks, and so our committee become involved along with the NAACP. We went over there and set up a picket line of the Human Rights Committee and the NAACP. We became involved in a lot of that. Our committee consisted of white members, and we all went together, hand in hand.

When our Human Rights Committee was growing strong, there was lots of activity going on in the NAACP. So we put recommendation from the committee to the rank and file and became a lifetime membership of the NAACP. The Human Rights Committee would coincide with the local NAACP, so that there would be three going to the NAACP national conventions from the local union.

My oldest brother was president of the NAACP in the sixties. He was on the Waterloo Human Rights Committee for several years; he was pretty active in the community and community work outside doing the union work, he was assistant chief steward during that time in the union, too.

Community civil rights activity by Local 46 reflected an alliance between moderate blacks in Robert Burt's circle, Charles Pearson's militant group, and antiracist whites. By working together, they broke down discrimination in the neighborhood of the plant and helped to turn the local NAACP chapter into an activist organization.

Charles Pearson

Right around the plant was very racist. Hollenbeck was the person that set up to have them break the racial barrier around the plant. We picked one tavern, that the guy said he would not serve blacks regardless, and went in. Four whites and four blacks goes into the tavern; the whites goes in first and we came in afterwards, and as we came in we ordered a beer and a sandwich. The waitress began to serve us when the owner came out of the back and said no, you couldn't serve them. A white stepped up and said, "Well if you can't serve them, we won't eat here either." And they walked out. OK. Then we walked out, go down to the local, about a block and a half from the tavern. Hollenbeck sets up and says, "OK, let's tell the chief steward and the president what we're going to do: we're going to bring charges with the State's Attorney." We brought charges, they found the place guilty, and charged them one hundred dollars, which was the maximum.

So the guy said he still wouldn't serve. So we started packing the place with more blacks and more blacks, and when we left packinghouse workers would also leave, so he was losing business both ways. Finally he said, "To hell with it, I'll go ahead and serve!" So he started serving us, and the business turned out to be very congenial.

We couldn't break the barrier if we went in to break it alone. All you had to do was say, this didn't happen. Now, here's four blacks and four whites, we go in. They were witnessing that this did happen.

After we went in that tavern, we set up what they called a "caravan." At that time it wasn't any black businesses along 4th street, and you had trouble eating or drinking. So we set up a caravan, and the caravan would say, spot one, we're going in, and we're going in as a mixed group. They knew that one tavern in front of the packinghouse had been sued, so they began to serve, but they would serve, you know, sloppy like. So we got a couple of guys who was really dynamic on pinball, and put a lot of games up there. That lasted for maybe six weeks, and the barrier broke.

There was no organization at the time—NAACP, church groups, or civic group—fighting the racial barrier. This is why we came up with an anti-discrimination committee, and probably within the packinghouse there was more done racially in Local 46 than the NAACP or other civic organizations, until Annie got active in the NAACP, then we had a combination thing. If Annie needed the local, she had the local; if the local needed Annie, they had Annie.

I would say '56 or '57 [Local] 46 put the packet together. In order to bring the NAACP to do what we thought they should have been doing, they went on record at the coordinating council in the Black Hawk Labor Council that all Council members become members of the NAACP. Annie and all of us, that's the only way we could have got in office at the time.

The NAACP had always been professional people—doctors and lawyers, maybe a schoolteacher. Like in most places, they wasn't doing anything but saying, "I'm the president of the NAACP." There was no membership unless they were the people that was on the same professional level. Black grassroot people during that time, the NAACP was a taboo to them. They wouldn't touch it because of the leadership that was in control, until the union grabbed it by the horns and said, "This is what we're going to do." After that, the upper echelon, the people that had control of the NAACP in the past, fell away. That only gave her [Anna Mae Weems] more incentive to become as dynamic as she was. No one in that town ever did what Annie did as the head of the NAACP.

The hiring of Anna Mae Weems in 1954 was the result of the union's strong anti-discrimination activities in the plant. Weems in turn helped to galvanize the local to extend its activities beyond the packinghouse and to attack discrimination in the community. As president of the local NAACP and a leader in Local 46's Human Relations Committee, Weems personified the alliance between black packinghouse workers and a local civil rights movement.

Anna Mae Weems

NAACP was a clique. They were black and they weren't concerned about welfare just as long as they had their coffee club. If you go to them they'd say, "Oh, we'll check it out." The man who was over it was a doctor who was in with the white folks. There was levels of decency around here. I mean, if you weren't in with the doctor and his group you wasn't worthy.

I started going to the NAACP and complaining. I asked everybody and said, "If you don't like what's going on, let's get together and let's move them out." So we voted them out of office and I took over.

When I was in the NAACP I thought that NAACP was the only organization that could get the rights for black people, and so we got them organized. Well we needed something outside of the city to help us keep in tune with what's going on nationwide as well as locally, so we thought that the best thing to do was to unite the two together—UPWA with the NAACP. So as I got into the union—I got my job, I joined the union—I also got to be chairman of the Human Relations Committee and president of the NAACP. I just merged the functions together.

We asked them [Local 46] to pass a mandate which said we should be involved with discrimination, advancement of black rights. That passed. Then we went to the regional UPWA convention and we got that same mandate passed, and then went to the national UPWA and got that mandate passed. Then we came back and used the NAACP as far as it could go, and then the UPWA took the rest.

A major focus of local civil rights organizing was boycotts of stores where blacks could shop but could not work or eat at lunch counters. Pickets would be drawn from the NAACP and white and black members of Local 46.

We did the National Dairy Farm Store. We did the A & P stores. We did Iowa Public Service utilities. We did places people shopped. Woolworth's, we had a counter sit-in.

We felt that since we were a union and one of the major companies, we wanted to make sure that we tried to do things that would be to the advantage and to the promotion of goodwill in this community. We didn't try to go in just to stir up trouble, we'd try to go in and create jobs.

We would have to spring a surprise on them. You don't call and say, "I'm going to picket you tomorrow." We'd meet with them and then we would show up the next morning, usually on a Friday, and the weekend. We'd have cars out there taking people to another place to shop.

Jimmy Porter, who started working at Rath in 1954, was swept up in the union's civil rights activity and became one of its most prominent activists on this issue.

Jimmy Porter

I applied and got a job at Rath. [Laughing] Oh hell, that was the greatest change of my life. Rath was unbelievable. I had never had the experience that I had when I went into Rath. Number one, black folk were in leadership capacity within their union. The other thing is, until 1954 a black woman had never been directly hired into the Rath plant. They were hired as janitors and then they transferred into the main plant. After 1954 the International put a stop to that; they hired their first black women. That happened in May and I went there the twenty-eighth of June 1954. I tell you, it was the beginning of my life all over again.

I had known most of the founders. I had known Mr. Lasley who had moved on to Chicago working for the International, I knew the Bob Robertsons, I knew the Chuck Pearsons, I knew the Isadore Pattersons. I knew all of these giants of the labor movement that was black, and when I went to Rath, the first thing I wanted to do is get involved because they were my idols. I saw where I could make a difference. It offered me an opportunity that I never dreamed I would have before.

My mentor, my idol, a guy named Chuck Pearson, schooled us good. He was a little bit radical. I must admit that we were a little bit more active than the norm, but at that time Rath was resistant to the union. It was not something that the Rath company felt they had to accept. The union was saying that we are here to stay, and there are things we are going to get regardless of what the cost is.

I became heavily involved for the next eighteen years. I was elected to an executive office as trustee in October 1955. Rath's gave me an opportunity to broaden my education. I traveled to conventions, got a chance to go to school; summer months got into a lot of industrial relations, management, union relations; attended a lot of seminars on my own. Most people didn't do it because you didn't get paid for it.

They started raising hell that the company wasn't hiring black people other than in two or three departments. We started having people who had seniority ask for transfers, and see how they were treated. Those new departments, black folk had never worked in before. When we had those first ten black women in, they said "Look, we're gonna walk out if they bring 'em in here." The company said, "Go ahead and walk out. When you walk out, you won't ever walk back in."

I never felt as a company policy I was ever discriminated against because of race. Unusual. I knew foremen who tried to run that bullshit game of race. But Rath's would fire your butt in a minute based upon that. But let me make sure I keep qualifying this. Management had some people working for them who was no worse than some of those from Mississippi. In fact, some of them were from Mississippi. We stood on their asses, not for their feeling but their behavior. We didn't give a damn where they're from, if they keep their shit out behind that door. Once they got inside that door we have them adhere to management policies. It was only because of that something was done.

They [white union members] gave us as much support outside as we could expect. Now the big problem with them was when we said, "Now look within your household." Oh shit. It's easier to kill tigers in Africa than to shoot cats in your own backyard.

Porter quickly became involved in community civil rights activity initiated by Local 46.

There was a young lady named Anna Mae Weems who had got hired about a month before I did. She was one of the first black women to be hired directly into the plant. Mrs. Weems took the union and took this town and turned it upside down, and we don't ever want to forget that.

To the stress and sometime resentment from a lot of our rank and filers, our union as a union went on record to fight discrimination. We started filing charges against merchants by them not serving black folk; first time we've ever won. The union became very much involved in public accommodations, appointments, employment beyond the doors of the packinghouse, affirmative action. She ran that for probably the next eight or ten years.

The union moved this town, and we began to pick up some support from other unions. The UAW came. It was placed in a position where it too could fight because someone else was blazing. The Black Hawk Union Council, which all the affiliated unions was a member of, became involved, and not only just affirmative action but in the total aspect of social concerns. A lot of people would volunteer to do these things. Hell, I would leave home every morning at eight o'clock and get back at midnight. It gave me an opportunity to grow.

A [human rights] committee used to meet two or three times a week to discuss what were we going to do, not only outside but also within our own plant, too. Just so many could serve because so much lost time would be involved. There were days when Mrs. Weems didn't work at all, there were days when I didn't work at all, and the union paid us. We had a strong Civil Rights Committee.

I recall when they would not serve us around Rath and downtown. There were a couple of cases the union took to court. We had a case where a person escaped, if I can use that term, and came here from Mississippi. One of them was fighting extradition—the union ran in and gave them a hand, was able to resist it. We went to the schools and started moving on them because they did not have black teachers. People would advertise for housing to be sold, when black folks would show up all of a sudden the place was rented. We start setting people up to have a white member to go in there and check, and have a black person to go in and take them to court. We had the same thing happen in taverns. Person would go in there and he says, "Look, all my tables are reserved." Then we'd have another person would go in there and he says, "Have a seat," and have those white people testify that this did happen to them. Even some paying a hell of a price to their neighbors as being traitors to their own race. The union had people who would do that.

It was a requirement, it was mandatory, that if you was an executive board member, you had to belong to the NAACP. Can you believe that? We had some white cats that would rather go to hell than let it be known that he was a member of the NAACP. But that was a mandate. And if you didn't, you got the hell off there.

Even though it was a great movement, don't ever forget I was still black. Don't ever forget that. There had never been a black person elected as president. There had been two including myself held the second highest position. There had never been a black person as high as chief steward. It was like a gentleman's agreement, if a white person want to serve here, a black person would go and serve here. But because it was so much greater than what I had been used to, that was something that I was willing to accept and work to eliminate.

Until Dr. King and our children came on the scene, we measured ourselves by how far we had come. It was only during the civil rights movement, especially when that "Black and Beautiful" came out, I stopped looking back how far I had come, and started thinking, "Damn, why should I settle for second-best?"

The policies of the International union were an asset to activists like Porter. While "it was up to the local people to say this is what's hurting me here," as Anna Mae Weems recalled, the International union provided valuable leverage for campaigns against local problems.

The union probably had the strongest policy on race than anything I have ever been involved with before or since. Helstein didn't walk on water. But I can say this, he could walk over racism and probably gave that union the kind of leadership that will never exist again. We would not sign a contract that didn't have the national policies, which no other union would do.

They never deviated from those policies, regardless of the cost to the organization. Our union was affiliated with every organization that was fighting discrimination: NAACP, Welfare Rights, Urban League. When Dr. King came on the scene our union, all over the United States, had to contribute a dollar per member to the well-being of that organization. In some places that went over like a fart in church. It just was not accepted, and we had a lot of people withdrew. In Mississippi they made such a big deal you were paying your dues to finance Martin Luther King. It was almost like you gotta take it or leave it, and we had some who would not take it.

We'd hold regional meetings, and once a year we all met together as a Human Rights [Committee] through the district, and once a year we met nationally. That was like going to the Congress—passing laws. Discrimination was part of the legislature that had to be spoken to. They knew the expectation from Helstein and Lasley and the rest of them.

143

The reason a lot of them had to do it, you had to report it. They wasn't just something to pass. Your district director was going to have to account for what you'd done. We had field reps. Every time he came in, he wrote a report on your ass and you were gonna hear it. They had such strong district directors here on civil rights, [Russell] Bull, then [Dave] Hart. If you didn't do it he was in your ass. That made a difference, hell of a lot of difference.

Charles Pearson also found the International union an important ally. However, he felt it was Local 46's militant rank and file that made the International tolerant of the Rath union's unorthodox strategies.

Charles Pearson

The International felt here was a local that was out there doing things. We were making things happen. When there may be trouble, the International had to be called. I would call and confirm that I was walking the plant out because of something, and then we would just go ahead. The backing was there, and the backing didn't have to be from them, the backing was just dynamic from within the plant.

My people on the international level was Russ Bull, Russ Lasley, [Charles] Hayes. There was a couple more guys there within that structure I was affiliated with one way or another, through Hollenbeck carrying me in the back door, or meeting some place to have a drink. I knew those were dynamic leaders within the union structure, and I guess my unorthodox method of unionism was the reason that they stayed touching base with me.

Pearson was not perturbed by accusations of Communist influence within the UPWA. To him, these charges reflected efforts to deflate the UPWA's dynamism.

I thought that they would use these tactics against the UPWA for the simple reason they were into dynamic organizing, and they were getting a job done. Only time the word Communism come up, when a local got to the point of being energetic like we were. Now see, I've heard that about Lowell, and I tried to dig, where is this Communist they're talking about. They talked about him being a Communist, and he had turned that local around with leadership. He had seen this guy is from down South and he can pull the blacks in this package, and this guy here is a farmer and he's got those guys over here, and he pulled us all together as a unified front.

They said Lowell was a Communist. Now if Lowell was a Communist, myself, Annie, Jimmie, all of them would have been labeled as a Communist. Out of all of them I think I'm the only one ever been labeled. The label just didn't mean anything for the simple reason, it was somebody just saying it; it wasn't carrying me before any type of hearing or anything. If I had to go before some kind of a hearing board, I might have felt differently.

Like Pearson, Jimmy Porter viewed accusations that the UPWA was Communist-dominated as a reflection of its responsiveness to rank-and-file union members and its commitment to advancing the interests of working people and minorities.

Jimmy Porter

We was branded as a Communist outfit, especially among white America, by saying that our head of organization was a Jew, the next one was a black guy, the next one a Canadian, and then a white guy was way down here. That had never happened in any union.

Here, a person say, "If you let all those Communist-believing folk stay out of here, there would be a better feeling here." Yeah, it might be but my black ass would be over yonder in that corner that you had relegated me to. So by damning them, you're actually making Communist heroes. You giving the Communists credit for what I look at as being democratic. You see what I'm saying? God damn, if this is Communism, don't ever let it die!

I believe that the organization was the most democratic organization that has ever come this way. Everybody it disagreed with it didn't feel any need to destroy, and everything that was a sin, didn't have to make it a crime. If you stay on your side of the fence and respect mine, we can coexist. And I tell you what, if you want to borrow my ax and I borrow your shovel, we still can exist. We don't have to dig into each other, but we can dig space enough to grow. I really believe that's what we was trying to do. I can respect people who thinks different than I do. But we are committed to the same thing. You want a good America, you want a good world, I do too. We're just going a different direction to get it. You say we're committed to the same thing, good, then we can argue over methods because that becomes a matter of opinion.

The rank and file ran the union. Not only did it run the union here, it ran it at the district level and at the national level. And those guys always had to worry about whether they were going to have a job and that came up every year. As I look back over it, maybe it was too democratic.

Overall, I saw action. I saw practice rather than preaching. I shall never forget that. It didn't only speak to blacks. It spoke to women. It spoke to oppressed people. It spoke to Jews. Even in its best days it never said, "Look, we got skill, we only be concerned about ourselves." Its biggest movement was beyond the doors of the packinghouse. It went ahead and faced 'em, and for all practical reasons was destroyed in the process. But it didn't back up.

The experiences of packinghouse workers in Local 46 left a long-lasting impact on their lives and commitment to social justice. Ada Tredwell was a civil rights activist in the community as well as the Rath plant in the 1960s. After leaving Rath in the mid-1970s, Tredwell worked as an educator and administrator at the African Palace Center (later called the Martin Luther King Center) in Waterloo's black community.

Ada Tredwell

I was really active in the YWCA, and the YWCA would rival the union in its activities trying to improve racial conditions in Waterloo. The YWCA was close to the black area, and they had lots of black young people coming to the YWCA for swimming and those kinds of activities. There was no other place offered this opportunity for black youth.

Their policy was this organization is for women and girls, regardless of color. They tried to abide by that. Of course there was opposition, even from some of the members of the board. For instance, when they wanted to open up the swimming pool for blacks there was opposition. But with courage that pool was open; the only place blacks could swim outside of the Cedar River was at the YWCA. They would hold activities in schools, like the Girl Reserves, and they would include black girls in that activity. I don't think they were involved in any sit-ins or anything like that, but all their activities that could be, were integrated. They probably were the first institution that really had black people serve on their board, which was another indication of what they were about.

I had gone to the march in Washington in 1963. When I came back we organized a group called the Citizens' Committee, and the Citizens' Committee was really an arm of the NAACP but we were strictly political. Now, the Citizens' Committee, the Local 46 civil rights committee, and the NAACP then were probably the most influential organizations in terms of changing things in Waterloo interracially, because once you get into politics, you can maneuver some people in order to get the vote. We had an all-black ticket. This black ticket was so threatening to whites. We knew we could not win, but the idea was to say that I'm not satisfied with what you're doing. This was kind of like a protest vote.

After leaving meatpacking, Charles Pearson utilized the training he had received in Local 46 in a succession of occupations. He was forced to leave Rath in 1958 to serve time in prison for murder. As a condition of his parole, he relocated to Peoria, Illinois. He operated a grocery store for a short period of time, labored at the

Hiram Walker distillery, and worked for the city of Peoria as a troubleshooter with local youth gangs. At the time of the interview, he was organizing public housing tenants.

Charles Pearson

My brother ran a business there in Waterloo, we had a nightclub. I killed a man in the nightclub. They gave me the least time they could for the crime, just so when I come back there was no more affiliation with the packing-house.

When I go to Fort Madison [a state prison] there were three areas that blacks didn't work. That was Mount Pleasant, which was a place for the mentally sick, the kitchen, and the tailor shop. So guys were talking that the tailor shop didn't have any blacks in it, and the kitchen didn't, so would I go and talk to the associated warden. If you got a gripe or a complaint you carried it to the associated warden. I went to the associated warden. This all come out of my union concept. This is why they asked me if I would do it.

I came back from prison, went to work for the city here in Peoria. The city hired me as a troubleshooter; they were having problems with gangs, and had a federal program, so the city hired 13 ex-cons to deal with gangs. Problems, gang-related or anything like that, they would shoot me in there. In '75 the housing authority was basically all white, and the city sent us in there to prepare to break the barrier. It's the strategy of [Local] 46 which carried me through four years of city [employment].

I can look back and say I'm happy. That union gave me the concept of leadership. If you was going to be here a few days, you could see me operating within housing. It all goes back to the local. I use the same strategies against housing, and right now I got housing turning where they're going to give to the people what they got coming. [Looking through papers] Now those grievances will be worked on tomorrow. I use the same tactics that I used when I was with the local. The good feeling of that is, like this woman here, housing owed her some money, and I'm going to get it for her, and there's several of them there that's going through the same concept. Here's a woman say, I need a bigger apartment because of my children. When I get that apartment for her, then my work will have been taken care of.

Conclusion

These powerful testimonies highlight the centrality of packinghouse work to the economic vitality and political advances of black America in the twentieth century. In many important ways, the packinghouse workers in this book truly were the "strength of their community."

Reading the oral histories with these men and women is one of the best ways to gain an understanding of their economic, political, and organizational contributions, as well as an appreciation of their particular outlook on American society. These ordinary people, most of whom spent their entire lives laboring in the meatpacking industry, are the ones whose stories are rarely recorded. In only a few cases did the interviewees in this collection rise to the sort of prominent positions in the labor movement that enabled their careers to be documented in paper records. In addition to providing factual information that ordinarily would be unavailable, these oral interviews provide unique access to the "horizontal" linkages in the life histories of their subjects, between episodes and experiences that traditional documentary sources generally distort beyond recognition or do not reveal.

Rowena Moore's life provides a good of example of the benefits of oral history. She does not appear in the official records of the UPWA until the 1950s, when she became a union officer in the Omaha Armour local, attended union conferences, and participated in her local anti-discrimination committee. Moore's more recent experiences are also documented in various Omaha newspapers because of her efforts to establish a historic memorial for Malcolm X. Based on these sources, without having the insights gained through oral history, it would seem logical to conclude (incorrectly) that it was her experiences in the United Packinghouse Workers of America that led to her activism around civil rights issues.

Moore's narrative provides a significantly different picture from that found in the written sources. From her perspective, it was the contact she had as an adolescent with black women's club activists that shaped her subsequent commitments as an NAACP member, union activist, and supporter of Malcolm X's mature political philosophy. Her experience as a community activist in the 1930s and early 1940s, and the black clubwomen's influence upon her, is conspicuously absent from the written record. Moreover, the influence of this early episode on Moore's activist trajectory cannot be derived from the written documentation about her life in the period following World War II. Both the basic facts about Moore's life and the "horizontal" links between different dimensions of her experiences are accessible through her oral narrative alone.

Taken collectively, these interviews provide a number of important insights into the black urban experience in twentieth-century America. Moore's story is only one of many examples of civil rights activism by working-class blacks many years before Martin Luther King Jr. and the Montgomery Bus Boycott riveted America's attention on Jim Crow segregation. Efforts to end discrimination in the workplace spilled over into community civil rights protests during and after the Second World War and placed the UPWA firmly in the civil rights camp long before a national movement took shape. Consequently, in the mid-1950s the UPWA was the first union that "joined hands" with King and the Southern Christian Leadership Conference, while, as Charles Hayes recalled, "other unions were remaining aloof from that movement."

Packinghouse workers were at the center of an urban, labor-based struggle for civil rights that grew out of the CIO organizing of the Depression decade, received new impetus during the war years, and flourished in the 1940s and 1950s. Only dimly apparent in newspaper accounts, official union records, and institutional archives, campaigns like those waged by Sam Parks to desegregate a Goldblatt's lunchroom on Chicago's near southside and Charles Pearson's efforts to integrate the taverns surrounding Rath's Waterloo plant form an important part of the history of black activism at mid-century. Especially significant is the way membership in a national union like the UPWA gave black workers in more remote locations the crucial leverage and resources they needed to challenge long-standing and deeply rooted inequalities. The Fort Worth narratives of Frank Wallace, Eddie Humphrey, and Mary Salinas show how local activists could ally with workers thousands of miles distant and acquire power disproportionate to their relatively small numbers in their own plant or community. Of course, in Fort Worth, cafeteria and locker room desegregation produced a tense, racially charged situation as well as a white backlash. The key point, though, is that the continued support of African American (and in this case, Mexican-American) workers for the union allowed the UPWA to aggressively move forward with the implementation of a civil rights program in one of the more inhospitable areas of the South.

The integral connections between black rights and women's rights are apparent from these interviews. Black men encouraged participation in union affairs by black women such as Virginia Houston and supported their efforts to overcome employment discrimination. In Waterloo, where company practice restricted black women to custodial jobs, Ada Tredwell recalled that "the black men wanted us out of there" and given "the same kind of opportunity that other women had." Black women who sought union support for efforts to end workplace discrimination against them found ready allies among the black men.

The activities of these black men and women was informed by a racialized class consciousness and an acute awareness of the differences between themselves and the black professional class within their communities. These differences emerged graphically in conflicts over the direction of local NAACP chapters in the 1950s. A belief by packinghouse workers that it was best for the black community to advance in a collective manner, employing confrontational tactics when necessary, distinguished them from the traditional NAACP leadership of doctors, lawyers, and businessmen. Chicago Armour worker Todd Tate called the NAACP a "silk-stocking," "tea sipping" organization that operated in a world far removed from ordinary working people—until UPWA members like Sam Parks led a working-class revolt within the local branch. In Waterloo, Anna Mae Weems described the local NAACP as a "clique" of professionals who "weren't concerned about welfare just as long as they had their coffee club." That was the case until, as Charles Pearson recalled, "the union grabbed it by the horns and said, 'This is what we're going to do.'" Far more so than traditional black middle-class leaders, packinghouse workers were committed to improving their communities by transforming the racial and economic status quo.

A powerful work ethic was an integral component of the working-class outlook of these men and women. Robert Burt proudly boasted that in "forty-three years I cannot recall I took a day off." In Kansas City, William Raspberry's belief in the work ethic led him to endorse Booker T. Washington's philosophy of uplift through skilled labor and individual endeavour. "I saw the wisdom in that," he recalled. "See, for a long time in the packinghouse I was making more money than most professionals." Even men like Philip Weightman, Frank Wallace, and Charles Hayes, who graduated from the shop floor to full-time, well-paid careers within the union bureaucracy, regarded their positions with a mixture of pride and responsibility. Rather than distance themselves from their constituencies, all three men utilized their posts to help other workers realize their "right to participate in the fullness of American life."

Among blacks, the work ethic did not induce conservatism. Indeed, quite the contrary was true; the righteousness of their toil legitimated demands for economic and social justice, for their rights as workers and as black Americans. Like Virginia Houston, who bluntly said that "work didn't bother me," it was inequality, injustice, and discrimination against those who worked so hard that instilled in black packinghouse workers their fierce determination to secure social equality. William Raspberry saw no contradiction between endorsing Washington's philosophy and using his position in the Kansas City labor movement to force the UAW to allow blacks onto the automobile assembly line.

Philip Weightman's story, which opens this book, testifies to how a powerful work ethic, along with the experience of discrimination at work and in the community, stimulated activism against class exploitation and racial discrimination. Although able to educate himself and secure critical employment skills through diligence and a degree of luck, Weightman always remained acutely aware of how race delimited his opportunities. A "company man" for many years because of a destructive encounter as a youth with the discriminatory practices of a labor organization, he nonetheless proved willing to join a union when confronted with the capricious character of managerial authority. Stunned by the sudden dismissal of a coworker, Weightman dramatically joined the CIO. As he explained to a supervisor, "You can do that to any of us. If I can do anything about it, you ain't going to do that to me nor no one else." For Weightman and the other workers in this book, unionism and collective action were integral components of their efforts to secure dignity at work and status in American society. The UPWA's brand of militant industrial unionism was the best means to fight against discrimination and to obtain power in their communities.

The rich contours of the lives and outlook of these black men and women emerge most clearly through their own words, through the recording of oral history. The narratives link dimensions of their lives usually treated separately in the books and articles written by historians and other academics. The oral histories reveal nuances and complications in the ideologies of working-class blacks that are generally truncated in synthetic, interpretive accounts. It is with their words, their subjective perceptions and experiences, that our exploration of race and the black experience in twentieth-century America must commence.

Appendix

SUMMARY CHART OF INTERVIEWS AND THEMES

Most of the interviews in this book are part of the UPWA Oral History Project. Included as well are a few additional interviews conducted by Rick Halpern and Roger Horowitz. Tapes of all these interviews are deposited in the Archives Reading Room, State Historical Society of Wisconsin, 816 State Street, Madison WI 53703.

The following chart lists the names of all the UPWA Oral History Project interviewees. They are classified by their primary urban area of residence and the packinghouse where they spent most of their working career. For those few who were not packinghouse workers but were interviewed for other reasons, the place of residence is listed as "other." Union staff members who were not packinghouse workers are designated as union staff. The miscellaneous category includes five interviewees who did not fit elsewhere in the chart for various reasons.

To aid the researcher, there are several designations on the chart to provide information at a glance on each interviewee. These are as follows:

*	union founder
B	black
W	white
M	Mexican-American
AD	anti-discrimination
WA	women's activities
IP	internal politics
SF	shop-floor dynamics
TN	tape number

The sex of interviewees can be deduced from their first names. The first column following the names lists each interviewee's racial background. The next four columns indicate whether the interview contains worthwhile material on the subjects of anti-discrimination, women's activities, internal politics, and shop-floor dynamics, respectively. The last column indicates the tape numbers where the recordings of the interviews may be found. A discussion of the information available in each subject category follows the chart.

	W/B/M	AD	WA	IP	SF	TN
AUSTIN, MN						
Hormel						
Winkels, John*	W			x		36–37
Winkels, Casper*	W				x	38–39
Halligan, Lyman*	W	x		x		43–44
Casey, Marie*	W		x			45–46
MacAnally, James	W				x	40–41
Sissel, Rollo	W				x	42
Losey, Paul	W				x	97–99
Shatek, Richard	W				x	97–99
Taylor, Dave	W				x	97–99
Johnson, Bob	W	x				97–99
Godfredsen, Svend*	W	x	x	x	x	143–150
Other						
Rasmussen, Paul	W			x		281–283
CEDAR RAPIDS, IA						
Wilson						
Lange, Ray	W					104–107
Townsend, Louise	W					110–112
Hammond, Jeanette	W					110–112
Fields, Magnolia	B	x			x	118–119
Zarudsky, Helen	W					108–109
Carr, Earl	B	x				113–115
Rowena, Lester	W					104–107
Hlavacek, Frank	W				x	104–107
Tickal, Louis*	W				x	104–107
Blumenshine, Don*	W				x	102–103
Melsha, Stella*	W					100–101
Melsha, Jack*	W					100–101
Fetter, Tony	W	x	x	x	x	120–122
Achenbach, Lloyd*	W				x	116–117
Other						
Gibson, Viola	B	x				141–142
CHICAGO, IL						
Armour						
March, Herbert*	W	x		x		1–2
						293–298
Norman, Milton	B	x			x	19–22
Samuel, James	B					19–22
Tate, Todd	B	x		x	x	11–12
						19–22
						23–25

	W/B/M	AD	WA	IP	SF	TN
Saunders, Richard*	B	x		x	x	11–12
						19–22
Swift						
Starr, Vicky*	W		x	x	x	234–236
Weightman, Philip*	B	x		x	x	284–292
Wilson						
Hayes, Charles	B	x		x	x	151–153
Collins, Annie J.	B					11–12
Parks, Sam	B	x		x	x	30–31
Independent Plants						
Wyatt, Addie	B	x	x	x		54–56
Taylor, Rosalie	B					15–16
Allen, Ercell	B					15–16
Vaughn, Jesse*	B			x	x	32–33
						299–300
Pierce, Eunetta	B	x	x		x	13–14

CUDAHY, WI
Patrick Cudahy

	W/B/M	AD	WA	IP	SF	TN
Nielsen, Harold	W	x		x		3–5
Tarnowski, Leona	W		x			34
Thoenes, Ervin*	W	x				6–35
Becker, Joe*	W	x				6

EAST ST. LOUIS, IL
Armour

	W/B/M	AD	WA	IP	SF	TN
Davenroy, William*	W	x				214–216
Madakitis, John*	W			x	x	220–223
Condellone, John*	W			x	x	220–223
Nash, William	B	x				209–211
Miller, Curtis	B					219
Peoples, Clyde	B	x				217–218
Swift						
Randall, Blackie	W					212–213

FORT WORTH, TX
Armour

	W/B/M	AD	WA	IP	SF	TN
Wallace, Frank*	B	x		x	x	75–78
Niedholdt, Kenneth	W				x	94–96
						191
Salinas, Mary	M	x	x	x	x	85–88
Jones, Hattie	W					89–90
Williams, L. C.	B	x				82–84
Humphrey, Eddie	B	x		x		79–81

	W/B/M	AD	WA	IP	SF	TN
Stockyards						
McCafferty, Charles B.	W	x		x		91–93
KANSAS CITY, MO						
Armour						
Block, Finis*	B	x			x	247–249
Fischer, Charles R.*	W	x		x		263–266
Krasick, Thomas*	W					275–277
Isom, Nevada	B				x	261–262
Houston, Virginia	B	x	x			278–280
Wilson						
Bailey, Walter*	B	x				273–274
Raspberry, William	B	x		x		250–253
Cudahy						
Simmons, Marian	B	x	x	x	x	254–260
Other						
Krasick, Ann	W					275–277
OMAHA, NB						
Armour						
Romano, Fred*	W			x		185–186
Peterson, Nels*	W			x		162–163
Watson, Betty	W		x			166–168
Dappen, Emerson	W			x		157–159
Moore, Rowena	B	x	x	x		175–178
Swift						
Myers, Vic	W	x		x		154–156
Graham, Max	W	x	x	x	x	182–184
Early, Homer*	B	x				160–161
Harris, James C.*	B	x		x	x	172–174
Fletemeyer, George*	W	x		x	x	187–190
Cassano, Herb*	W			x		169–171
Cudahy						
Balters, Steve	W					164–165
Poe, Darryl*	W	x			x	179–181
Mason, Walt*	W	x			x	179–181
Dappen, Jeannette	W					157–159
Other						
Fletemeyer, Francis	W					187–190
ST. JOSEPH, MO						
Armour						
Chambers, Clyde*	W					239–241
Thompson, Buford	B	x			x	271–272

	W/B/M	AD	WA	IP	SF	TN
Crowley, Eugene	B	x	x		x	242–244
Carter, Marjorie	B	x	x		x	242–244
Webster, William	B				x	245–246

SOUTH ST. PAUL, MN
Cudahy

Giannini, Henry*	W			x	x	57–59
						67–70

Swift

Nolan, William*	W			x	x	57–59
						60–63

Armour

Wicke, Chris*	W					57–59
						71–72
Cooper, Jake	W					73–74
Winters, Don	W					57–59

Other

DeBoer, Harry	W					59
Hall, Douglas	W			x		64–66

SIOUX CITY, IA
Cudahy

Shuck, Jenny*	W		x	x		207–208
Nolan, Bruce*	W			x	x	204–206
Holbrook, Grant*	W			x	x	204–206

Armour

Wensel, Clyde*	W			x		194–196
Edwards, Alvin*	W					199–200
Edwards, Mary*	W		x			199–200
Davis, Sam	B	x				201–203

Swift

Hilsinger, James*	W					192–193
Callender, Loren	W					197–198

WATERLOO, IA
Rath

Lamb, Goldie			W			140
Bremmer, Lucille	W		x	x	x	123–125
Jones, Viola	W				x	127–128
Porter, James	B	x				135–136
Pearson, Charles	B	x		x	x	224–227
Dietz, Everett	W					126
Dietz, Vernon*	W					126

	W/B/M	AD	WA	IP	SF	TN
Taylor, Lyle	W	x	x	x		133–134
Mueller, Charles	W	x	x	x	x	139
						232–233
Tredwell, Ada	B	x	x		x	228–229
Weems, Anna Mae	B	x	x		x	137–138
Schrader,						
Velma Otterman*	W		x		x	131–132
Burt, Robert*	B	x			x	129–130
						230–231

UNION STAFF

Alston, Harry	B	x				51–53
Cotton, Eugene	W					28–29
Dolnick, Norman	W			x		26–27
Fischer, Charles	W	x				49–50

MISCELLANEOUS

Hill, Herbert	W	x		x		8–10
Lefkowitz, Hy	W				x	237–238
Pittman, A. J.*	W			x		267–270
Schultz, Robert*	W					7
						17–18
Prosten, Jesse*	W	x		x		47–48

Anti-discrimination

Among the richest areas explored in the oral history interviews are those pertaining to race relations in the packing industry in general and the civil rights activities of the UPWA in particular. All interviewees, both black and white, were asked about racial discrimination in hiring, job placement, and promotion before and after the establishment of the union. Likewise, segregation inside the plants and in the larger community forms an important concern in the interviews. The building of interracial solidarity during the PWOC era is explored in considerable detail in many of the oral histories, as are the early anti-discrimination efforts of the union. The changing racial composition of the packinghouse workforce during World War II and afterward is an important topic that receives much attention.

Anti-discrimination activity varied greatly by both geographic locale and by local union. Information about "A-D" activity initiated by local unions in the plant and in the community was solicited wherever possible. Similarly, the implementation of the International union's civil rights program, especially in the period following the 1948 strike, formed a key area of inquiry in interviews with union officials and local activists. The UPWA sought to cultivate ties with other civil rights groups throughout its existence. Interviewees often offered valuable recollections about their union's relationship with local NAACP branches and chapters of the Urban League. Since aggressive civil rights activities often clashed with the sensibilities of white unionists, interviewers sought information on the white workers' opinions of the union's anti-discrimination program. Especially interesting are the dramatic divergences between black and white views of the same phenomena.

Women's Issues

The experience of female packinghouse workers differed in many significant ways from that of males. Information about women's issues and concerns was consciously sought at every opportunity. Women tended to be concentrated in certain departments in the plant, and almost all of the interviews with women include descriptions of women's work itself. In general, women played only a minor role in the initial organization of PWOC locals. Often (but not always) traditionally female departments such as sausage and sliced bacon formed major obstacles to organization. However, several of the oral history interviews are with atypical female packinghouse workers who were early supporters of union organizing drives and who later emerged as leaders of the women in their plant. These interviews in particular explore the dynamics of female participation in the union.

Several interviews contain superb information on the specific problems facing women workers—sexual harassment, wage differentials, inequities involved in piecework, and so forth. Likewise, several interviews contain accounts about the organization of women's activities committees in the 1950s, as well as testimony about the other ways women organized to forward demands inside the union apparatus. The number of women employed in meatpacking increased over time, as did the proportionate number of black women in the industry. This trend began with World War II, and many interviewees comment on it. The project interviewed several black women who broke the color line in previously all-white departments. A major topic in almost all of the female interviews and in a good number of those with male stewards and local leaders is the impact of mechanization on women workers in the late 1950s and early 1960s. Women bore the burden of job displacement due to new technology, and in most local unions this led to protracted and bitter conflicts over the seniority system. Several interviews contain detailed accounts about the struggle over plant versus departmental seniority and over the related conflict which surrounded the merging of male and female seniority lists.

Internal Politics

One of the distinguishing features of the UPWA was its internal political diversity and democracy. The interviewees range widely in political outlook, from Communists on the left to strong conservatives on the right. There is a great deal of information on the role of the leftists in the union, primarily Communists but also Socialists, Trotskyists, and members of the Industrial Workers of the World (IWW). The interviews are particularly informative on the contribution of the Left to the initial formation of packinghouse local unions. The opinions of conservative interviewees on Communists and other leftists are especially important, as the vast majority of them do not exhibit the kind of anti-communism that took hold in other CIO unions. A number of key actors on opposite sides of the factional struggles of 1948 and 1954 were interviewed and provided invaluable personal recollections on their motives as well as sober reflections on their strategy and objectives. The interviewees also discuss the particular influence of UPWA president Ralph Helstein on the liberal atmosphere that prevailed inside the union.

Shop-Floor Dynamics

Virtually every packinghouse worker interviewee discusses his or her particular job and how it changed over time. The description of the work process
ranges from accounts of the transition from preunion to union conditions in
the 1930s and 1940s to the changes caused by new technology in the 1950s
and 1960s. In the better descriptions of shop-floor dynamics, the interviewees discuss the relationship in their departments between the work gang,
the stewards, and the supervisory personnel. Often these include extensive
and precise descriptions of job actions, ranging from informal slowdowns to
carefully planned stoppages. A few interviewees also describe the union
apparatus inside the plant, its internal lines of communication, relationships
between departmental stewards and the local union officers, and plantwide
job actions. The interviewers took care to solicit the opinions of packinghouse workers on the role they saw the union organization playing inside
the plant, especially its importance in securing initial support for the union.

Notes and References

The endnotes include only sources for direct quotations or specific numerical data. For full documentation, see Rick Halpern, *Down on the Killing Floor: Black and White Workers in Chicago's Packinghouses, 1904–1954* (Urbana, Ill.: University of Illinois Press, 1997), and Roger Horowitz, *"Negro and White, Unite and Fight!" A Social History of Industrial Unionism in Meatpacking, 1930–1990* (Urbana, Ill.: University of Illinois Press, 1997).

PREFACE

1. For more information see James A. Cavanaugh, "From the Bottom Up: Oral History and the United Packinghouse Workers of America," *International Journal of Oral History* 9 (February 1988).

CHAPTER I

1. Quoted in Studs Terkel, *Race: How Whites and Blacks Think and Feel about the American Obsession* (New York: New Press, 1992), 342.

2. First quotation from James R. Grossman, "A Dream Deferred: Black Migration to Chicago, 1916–1921" (Ph.D. diss., University of California–Berkeley, 1982), 6. Second quotation from Emmett J. Scott, "Letters of Negro Migrants of 1916–1918," *Journal of Negro History* 4 (October 1919): 457.

3. The experiences and recollections of black packinghouse workers in this book support an approach to African American history developed by Joe William Trotter Jr. In his first book, *Black Milwaukee: The Making of an Industrial Proletariat* (Urbana, Ill.: University of Illinois Press, 1985), Trotter argued that historians should abandon the older model of ghetto formation, which portrayed urban blacks as victims of discrimination. Instead, he advanced a paradigm that he termed "proletarianization," which emphasized the active creation of black urban communities by working-class blacks. The narratives of these books testify to the role played by packinghouse workers in the construction and cohesion of their communities.

4. First quotation from testimony by Robert Bedford in hearings of Judge Samuel Alschuler, June 20–23, 1919, 221, Federal Mediation and Conciliation Service Records, Record Group 280, National Archives Record Center, Suitland, Md. Second quotation from Ann Banks, ed., *First Person America* (New York: Norton, 1991; originally published 1980), 68.

5. Quotation from Banks, *First Person America*, 67–68.

6. Todd Tate interview, United Packinghouse Workers of America Oral History Project, State Historical Society of Wisconsin, Madison, Wis. [hereafter cited as UPWAOHP].

7. Temporary National Economic Committee, *Large-Scale Organization in the Food Industries*, Monograph No. 35, 76th Congress, 3rd Session (Washington, D.C.: Government Printing Office, 1940), 17.

8. Alma Herbst, "The Negro in the Slaughtering and Meat Packing Industry in Chicago," (Ph.D. diss., University of Chicago, 1930), 305.

9. James R. Barrett, *Work and Community in the Jungle: Chicago's Packinghouse Workers, 1894–1922* (Urbana, Ill.: University of Illinois Press, 1987), 22. John R. Commons, "Labor Conditions in Meat Packing and the Recent Strike," *Quarterly Journal of Economics* 19 (November 1904): 4.

10. Summner Slichter quoted in Sanford M. Jacoby, *Employing Bureaucracy: Managers, Unions, and the Transformation of Work in American Industry, 1900–1945* (New York: Columbia University Press, 1985), 20. For further discussion of the drive system, see Jacoby, 21–23, 190, 218–19, and 243.

11. Quotation from James R. Grossman, *Land of Hope: Chicago, Black Southerners, and the Great Migration* (Chicago: University of Chicago Press, 1989), 187.

12. John R. Commons, introduction to *History of Labor in the United States, 1896–1932*, ed. Don D. Lescohier and Elizabeth Brandeis (New York: Macmillan, 1935), 3:xxv.

13. Thomas in Banks, *First Person America*, 69.

14. Jesse Vaughn interviews, UPWAOHP.

15. Kenneth Neidholdt interview, March 20, 1986, UPWAOHP.

16. Mary Elizabeth Pidgeon, *The Employment of Women in Slaughtering and Meat Packing*, U.S. Department of Labor Women's Bureau Bulletin No. 88 (Washington, D.C.: Government Printing Office, 1932), 17, 37–41.

17. Alma Herbst, *The Negro in the Slaughtering and Meat-Packing Industry* (New York: Arno, 1971; originally published 1932), 77–78.

18. Quote from Herbst, *The Negro in the Slaughtering and Meat-Packing Industry*, preface.

19. Gertie Kamarczyk interview with Rick Halpern, December 5, 1987; Joe Zabritski interview with Rick Halpern, December 4, 1987.

20. Quotation from Jim Cole interview in Banks, *First Person America*, 67.

21. Quotations from Jesse Prosten interview, UPWAOHP. For Johnson's background, see Stephen Brier, "Labor, Politics, and Race: A Black Worker's Life," *Labor History* 23 (Summer 1982), 416–21.

22. Ercell Allen and Rosalie Taylor interview, UPWAOHP.

23. James C. Harris interview, UPWAOHP.

24. Charles R. Fischer interview, UPWAOHP. Darrel Poe and Walt Mason interview, UPWAOHP.

25. Richard Saunders quotation from Milton Norman, Richard Saunders, Todd Tate, and James Samuel interview, UPWAOHP.

26. Eddie Humphrey interview, UPWAOHP. "UPWA Self-Survey of Human Relations, 1948–49," United Packinghouse Workers of America Papers, Box 345, Folder 13, State Historical Society of Wisconsin, Madison, Wis. [hereafter cited as UPWA Papers].

27. Charles Pearson interview, UPWAOHP.

28. Ralph Helstein interview with Rick Halpern and Roger Horowitz, July 18, 1983. John Hope II, *Equality of Opportunity: A Union Approach to Fair Employment* (Washington, D.C.: Public Affairs Press, 1956).

29. The contract clause read, "The company agrees that it will give fair and reasonable consideration to any applicant or employee regardless of race, sex, color, creed, nationality, or membership in the Union."

30. Anna Mae Weems interview, UPWAOHP.

31. Nevada Isom interview, UPWAOHP.

32. Tate quotation from Annie Jackson Collins, Richard Saunders, and Todd Tate interview, UPWAOHP.

33. "Summary Fact Sheets Documenting Job Crisis in Meat Packing Industry," UPWA Papers, Box 175, Folder 5. UPWA membership figures for 1953 in UPWA Papers, Box 497, Folder 7. Figures for 1967 are from UPWA International Executive Board minutes, July 17, 1967, Ralph Helstein Papers, State Historical Society of Wisconsin, Madison, Wis. U.S. Department of Labor, *Industry Wage Survey: Meat Products* (Washington, D.C.: Government Printing Office, November 1963), 12. U.S. Department of Labor, *Industry Wage Survey: Meat Products* (Washington, D.C.: Government Printing Office, June 1984), 6.

34. Quotation from Todd Tate interview, UPWAOHP.

35. For a transcript of King's speech, see "The Fourth Annual Wage and Contract Conference and the Third National Anti-Discrimination Conference and the Third National Conference on Women's Activities," September 30–October 4, 1957, UPWA Papers, Box 526, 208–33.

36. Ralph Helstein interview, July 18, 1983.

CHAPTER 2

1. Lowell Washington interview with Rick Halpern, April 28, 1988.

2. Gertie Kamarczyk interview with Rick Halpern, December 15, 1987.

3. John Wrublewski interview with Rick Halpern, April 28, 1988.

4. Quotation from Ralph Helstein interview with Rick Halpern and Roger Horowitz, July 18, 1983.

5. Lowell Washington interview with Halpern.

6. Saunders in Richard Saunders, Todd Tate, and Annie Jackson Collins interview, UPWAOHP.

7. Quotation from Theodore V. Purcell, *The Worker Speaks His Mind on Company and Union* (Cambridge, Mass.: Harvard University Press, 1953), 176.

8. Herbert March interview, July 15, 1985, UPWAOHP. Kamarczyk interview with Halpern.

CHAPTER 3

1. In the following narrative, a December 10, 1987, interview with William Raspberry by Roger Horowitz has been combined with the UPWAOHP interview.

2. In the following narrative, a December 8, 1987, interview with Virginia Houston by Roger Horowitz has been combined with the UPWAOHP interview.

CHAPTER 4

1. See the following works for more information on the role of black club women. Darlene Clark Hine, *Hine Sight: Black Women and the Reconstruction of American History* (Brooklyn: Carlson Publishing, 1994). Stephanie J. Shaw, "Black Club Women and the Creation of the National Association of Colored Women," in *"We Specialize in the Wholly Impossible": A Reader in Black Women's History,* ed. Darlene Clark Hine, Wilma King, and Linda Reed. (Brooklyn: Carlson Publishing, 1995). Gerda Lerner, "Early Community Work of Black Club Women," *Journal of Negro History* 59 (April 1974). Anne Firor Scott, "Most Invisible of All: Black Women's Voluntary Associations," *Journal of Southern History* 56 (February 1990). Dorothy C. Salem, "To Better Our World: Black Women in Organized Reform" (Ph.D. diss., Kent State University, 1986).

CHAPTER 5

1. Spanish-speaking packinghouse workers referred to themselves as "Mexicans" regardless of their place of birth. In this chapter, the terms "Mexican" and "Mexican-American" are used interchangeably.

Further Reading

I. RACE, GENDER, AND UNIONISM IN THE MEATPACKING INDUSTRY

Banks, Ann, ed. *First Person America*. New York: Norton, 1980.

Brody, David. *The Butcher Workmen*. Cambridge, Mass.: Harvard University Press, 1964.

Cayton, Horace R., and George S. Mitchell. *Black Workers and the New Unions*. Chapel Hill: University of North Carolina Press, 1939.

Corey, Lewis. *Of Meat and Men: A Study of Monopoly, Unionism, and Food Policy*. New York: 1950.

Deslippe, Dennis A. "'We Had an Awful Time With Our Women': Iowa's United Packinghouse Workers of America, 1945–75." *Journal of Women's History* 5 (1993).

Fehn, Bruce. "'Power Concedes Nothing Without Demand': Women and Their Struggle for Equality in the Meatpacking Industry, 1900–1968." Ph.D. diss., University of Wisconsin–Madison, 1991.

———. "'Chickens Come Home to Roost': Industrial Reorganization, Seniority, and Gender Conflict in the United Packinghouse Workers of America, 1955–1966." *Labor History* 34 (1993).

Fogel, Walter A. *The Negro in the Meat Industry*. Philadelphia: Whorton School, 1970.

Halpern, Rick. *Down on the Killing Floor: Black and White Workers in Chicago's Packinghouses, 1904–1954*. Urbana, Ill.: University of Illinois Press, forthcoming 1997.

Hope, John, II. *Equality of Opportunity: A Union Approach to Fair Employment*. Washington, D.C.: Public Affairs Press, 1956.

Horowitz, Roger. *"Negro and White, Unite and Fight!" A Social History of Industrial Unionism in Meatpacking, 1930–1990*. Urbana, Ill.: University of Illinois Press, forthcoming 1997.

———. "'Where Men Will Not Work': Gender, Power, Space, and the Sexual Division of Labor in America's Meatpacking Industry, 1890–1990." *Technology and Culture* 37 (1996).

167

Kampfert, Arthur. "History of Unionism in Meatpacking." Typescript, copy available at the State Historical Society of Wisconsin, Madison, Wis., 1945.

Lynd, Alice, and Staughton Lynd, eds. *Rank and File: Personal Histories by Working-Class Organizers*. Boston: Beacon Press, 1973.

Pidgeon, Mary Elizabeth. *The Employment of Women in Slaughtering and Meat Packing*. U.S. Department of Labor Women's Bureau Bulletin No. 88. Washington, D.C.: Government Printing Office, 1932.

Warren, Wilson J. "The Limits of New Deal Social Democracy: Working-Class Structural Pluralism in Midwestern Meatpacking, 1900–1955." Ph.D. diss., University of Pittsburgh, 1992.

II. INDUSTRIAL UNIONISM IN MID-TWENTIETH-CENTURY AMERICA

Galenson, Walter. *The CIO Challenge to the AFL: A History of the American Labor Movement, 1935–1941*. Cambridge, Mass.: Harvard University Press, 1960.

Preis, Art. *Labor's Giant Step: Twenty Years of the CIO*. New York: Pioneer Press, 1964.

Zieger, Robert. *The CIO: 1935–1955*. Chapel Hill: University of North Carolina Press, 1995.

III. CHICAGO

Barrett, James R. *Work and Community in the Jungle: Chicago's Packinghouse Workers, 1894–1922*. Urbana, Ill.: University of Illinois Press, 1987.

Brier, Stephen. "Labor, Politics, and Race: A Black Worker's Life." *Labor History* 23 (1982).

Chicago Commission on Race Relations. *The Negro in Chicago: A Study of Race Relations and a Race Riot*. Chicago: CCRR, 1922.

Cohen, Lizabeth. *Making a New Deal: Industrial Workers in Chicago, 1919–39*. New York: Cambridge University Press, 1990.

Commons, John R. "Labor Conditions in Meat Packing and the Recent Strike." *Quarterly Journal of Economics* 19 (1904).

Drake, St. Clair, and Horace R. Cayton. *Black Metropolis: A Study of Negro Life in a Northern City*. New York: Harcourt, Brace & World, 1945.

Grossman, James R. *Land of Hope: Chicago, Black Southerners, and the Great Migration*. Chicago: University of Chicago Press, 1989.

———. "The White Man's Union: The Great Migration and the Resonance of Race and Class in Chicago, 1916–1922." In *The Great Migration in Historical Perspective: New Dimensions of Race, Class, and Gender*, ed. Joe William Trotter Jr. Bloomington, Ind.: Indiana University Press, 1991.

Halpern, Rick. "The Iron Fist and the Velvet Glove: Welfare Capitalism in Chicago's Packinghouses, 1921–1933." *Journal of American Studies* 26 (1992).

———. "Race, Ethnicity, and Union in the Chicago Stockyards, 1917–22." *International Review of Social History* 37 (1992).

Herbst, Alma. *The Negro in the Slaughtering and Meat-Packing Industry.* New York: Arno, 1971; originally published 1932.

Hirsch, Arnold. *The Making of the Second Ghetto.* New York: Cambridge University Press, 1985.

Newell, Barbara Warne. *Chicago and the Labor Movement: Metropolitan Unionism in the 1930s.* Urbana, Ill.: Univeristy of Illinois Press, 1961.

Ralph, James R., Jr. *Northern Protest: Martin Luther King, Jr., Chicago, and the Civil Rights Movement.* Cambridge, Mass.: Harvard University Press, 1993.

Slayton, Robert A. *Back of the Yards: The Making of a Local Democracy.* Chicago: University of Chicago Press, 1986.

Spear, Allan H. *Black Chicago: The Making of a Negro Ghetto.* Chicago: University of Chicago Press, 1967.

Street, Paul Louis. "Working in the Yards: A History of Class Relations in Chicago's Meatpacking Industry, 1886–1960." Ph.D. diss., State University of New York–Binghamton, 1993.

Tuttle, William. *Race Riot: Chicago in the Red Summer of 1919.* New York: Atheneum, 1970.

IV. KANSAS CITY

Atkinson, Eva Lash. "Kansas City's Livestock Trade and Packing Industry, 1870–1914: A Study in Regional Growth." Ph.D. diss., University of Kansas, 1971.

Greenbaum, Susan. *The Afro–American Community in Kansas City, Kansas.* Kansas City, Kans.: City of Kansas City, 1982.

League of Women Voters. *The Negro in Kansas City.* Kansas City, Mo.: League of Women Voters, 1944.

Martin, Asa. *Our Negro Population.* Kansas City, Mo.: Asa Martin, 1913.

Naismith, Clifford. "History of the Negro Population of Kansas City, Missouri, 1870–1930." Typescript, in Western Historical Manuscripts collection, University of Missouri–Kansas City, n.d.

National Urban League. *A Study of the Social and Economic Conditions of the Negro Population of Kansas City, Missouri.* Kansas City, Mo.: Urban League, 1946.

Painter, Nell Irvin. *Exodusters: Black Migration to Kansas after Reconstruction.* New York: Knopf, 1977.

Pearson, Nathan W. *Goin' to Kansas City.* Urbana, Ill.: University of Illinois Press, 1987.

Urban League of Kansas City. *The Negro Worker of Kansas City*. Kansas City, Mo.: Urban League, 1940.

———. *Housing Negro Families in Kansas City*. Kansas City, Mo.: Urban League, 1941.

Wilson, Noel Avon. "The Kansas City Call: An Inside View of the Negro Market." Ph.D. diss., University of Illinois, 1968.

V. FORT WORTH

Adedji, Moses. "Crossing the Colorline: Three Decades of the United Packinghouse Workers of America in the Trans-Mississippi West, 1936–1968." Ph.D. diss., North Texas State University, 1978.

Halpern, Rick. "Interracial Unionism in the Southwest: Fort Worth's Packinghouse Workers, 1937–1954." In *Organized Labor in the Twentieth Century South*, ed. Robert H. Zieger. Knoxville, Tenn.: University of Tennessee Press, 1991.

———. "Organised Labour, Black Workers, and the Twentieth Century South: The Emerging Revision." *Social History* 19 (1994).

Pate, J'Nell L. "Livestock Legacy: A History of the Fort Worth Stockyards Company, 1893–1982." Ph.D. diss., North Texas State University, 1982.

Talbert, Robert H. *Cowtown Metropolis*. Fort Worth: Texas Christian University Press, 1956.

VI. WATERLOO

Bergmann, Leola Nelson. *The Negro in Iowa*. Iowa City: University of Iowa Press, 1969; originally published 1948.

Bultena, Louis, and Harold Reasby. "Negro-White Relations in the Waterloo Metropolitan Area." Unpublished typescript, in UPWA Papers, Box 347, Folder 13, State Historical Society of Wisconsin, Madison, Wis., 1955.

Daly, John Marie. "History of Unionization: Waterloo, Iowa." Master's thesis, Creighton University, 1960.

Fehn, Bruce. "'The Only Hope We Had': United Packinghouse Workers Local 46 and the Struggle for Racial Equality in Waterloo, Iowa, 1948–1960." *Annals of Iowa* 54 (Summer 1995).

McCarty, H. H., and C. W. Thompson. "Meat Packing in Iowa." *Iowa Studies in Business* 12 (June 1933).

Stromquist, Shelton. *Solidarity and Survival: An Oral History of Iowa Labor in the Twentieth Century*. Iowa City: University of Iowa Press, 1993.

Index

Page numbers in italics indicate photographs.

171

The Authors

Rick Halpern teaches American history at University College London. In addition to numerous articles on race and labor, he is the author of *Down on the Killing Floor: Black and White Workers in Chicago's Packinghouses* (University of Illinois Press). Halpern chairs the seminar on Comparative Labour and Working Class History at the University of London's Institute of Historical Research. Currently he is working on a study of the southern sugar industry.

Roger Horowitz is Associate Director of the Center for the History of Business, Technology, and Society at the Hagley Museum and Library and teaches history at the University of Delaware. He is the author of *"Negro and White, Unite and Fight!" A Social History of Industrial Unionism in Meatpacking, 1930–1990* (University of Illinois Press). Horowitz also has published articles on World War II and the southern poultry industry. Currently he is examining the effect of military service on working-class Americans.